T0301765

THE TOXICOLOGIST
AS EXPERT WITNESS

THE TOXICOLOGIST AS EXPERT WITNESS

A Hint Book for Courtroom Procedure

Arthur Furst
University of San Francisco
San Francisco, California

CRC Press
Taylor & Francis Group
Boca Raton London New York

CRC Press is an imprint of the
Taylor & Francis Group, an **informa** business

CRC Press
Taylor & Francis Group
6000 Broken Sound Parkway NW, Suite 300
Boca Raton, FL 33487-2742

© 1997 by Taylor & Francis Group, LLC
CRC Press is an imprint of Taylor & Francis Group, an Informa business

No claim to original U.S. Government works

ISBN 13: 978-1-56032-531-4 (hbk)

Visit the Taylor & Francis Web site at
http://www.taylorandfrancis.com

and the CRC Press Web site at
http://www.crcpress.com

I would like especially to acknowledge my late wife, Florence Furst, librarian, editor of my scientific papers, and proofreader par excellence. She did encourage me to write this book.

CONTENTS

FOREWORD

If you are a toxicologist who intends to serve as an expert witness in a legal proceeding, you could not do yourself a better service than to spend a few serious hours with this book.

To the toxicologist with little or no experience with legal proceedings, the courtroom can seem like a minefield. Most fortunately, Dr. Furst's book is not an academic treatise. It is a *practical guide* for the forensic expert. To use an analogy, this is not a work about the history and theory of warfare; rather, it is a soldier's manual on how to survive and win on the battlefield.

Dr. Furst's book walks the toxicologist who would be an expert witness through the entire process. He begins properly by defining the concept and qualifications of the "expert"; discusses the proper way in which toxicologists must work with (and assist) the advocates who retain them; addresses how attorneys seek to prepare toxicologists for the battle at hand; notes key aspects of the deposition process, often a critical stage in the case for the expert toxicologist; and then informs the reader of what to expect from the trial itself, its actors, and its ramifications.

Now why would any sensible toxicologist try to play a role in this system without first getting a good lay of the land? Dr. Furst's book delivers that and more.

I also commend this work to all others who labor at the intersections of science and law, particularly judges, lawyers, legislators, and regulators. Powerful intellectual, social, economic, and political forces have bound law and science together in ways never envisioned decades ago. In courtrooms, legislative bodies, and regulatory agencies, we regularly depend on information from toxicologists to make decisions of profound significance. These decisions concern, among other things, the safety of the water we drink, the safety and efficacy of medications we take, and the risks we run by exposing our children and ourselves, at home and in the workplace, to hundreds of thousands of chemicals, natural and synthetic.

We have no choice but to confront and resolve these issues. We properly remain committed, moreover, to doing so in a manner consistent with our democratic principles. We will not always reach the "right" conclusion, but we should obviously strive for as much precision as possible. From toxicologists (and all other experts), we need competent, honest, and forthright assistance. It is important not only to the parties directly interested in some dispute, but for society at large.

Dr. Furst has made many significant contributions toward these ends as a prominent toxicologist, expert witness, and scholar. He clearly has his finger on the pulse. I thus heartily recommend his latest work to you.

Marc S. Klein, Esq.
Newark, New Jersey

PREFACE

A book on the expert witness, especially for the toxicologist, is justified on the basis of immediate need. As the world becomes more complex, a greater percentage of the present litigation than ever before is based on very technical subjects. There are more than a million synthetic chemicals in commerce. More and more chemicals are being introduced into our daily lives, and only a very few are being removed. Too few have been tested for all possible side effects (read: toxic effects). Even those agents not currently in use leave their legacy for years to come (e.g., DDT, PCBs, and asbestos). Throughout the nation, product liability and toxic tort cases are increasing at a phenomenal rate. A *toxic tort case* concerns a wrongful act that causes some injury to a person or property. The media play up every adverse effect of a chemical or physical agent with a sensational new article. In the past, a toxic tort case would involve an immediate injury from a specific exposure, for example, "Lye splattered in the face and some got into an eye; damage was done to the cornea." Such an injury could be seen and documented, and the amount of monetary compensation could then be determined.

In the last decade the term "toxic torts" has become quite a household word. This relatively new type of litigation has complicated the system, in that no longer is an individual or a specific lot of land involved. These days, court cases may include a large number of plaintiffs, possibly hundreds or thousands; there may also be hundreds of defendants. Harm caused by exposure to a substance may not manifest itself for a number of years; individual plaintiffs may not be able to display specific symptoms at the time of a trial. The claims for damage can be for a variety of pathologies, and all members of a suing population may not claim the same injury. As a result of actual or imagined exposure, more esoteric damages are now claimed, such as hyperactivity, difficulty in learning, future immunological impairment, neurological deficit, multiple chemical sensitivity, fear of cancer, emotional stress, and the like. Also to be considered is the individual who is exquisitely sensitive to a specific compound; often this person will seek monetary damage against the manufacturer of that agent.

A cancer phobia prevails in our society. In addition, many members of the public believe that all birth defects must be caused by some chemical exposure.

There are also many who believe that all exposures to a substance, especially if it is called "toxic," must by definition result in some injury that can be used to sue some group or another. On the other hand, there are too many actual cases in which a person has been exposed to a chemical that has resulted in some temporary or even permanent physiological or pathological damage; the toxicologist may be called upon to sort all this out.

It has been known for years that pregnant women are most vulnerable to having defective offspring if they are exposed to some noxious agent, or even some prescription drugs, especially in the first trimester. It is now also recognized that exposure of men to certain chemicals can result in defective sperm, or low or no sperm count, which in turn can and certainly will be associated with birth defects.

If "the dose makes the poison," how can a jury be made to understand and appreciate this concept? How should a toxicologist explain to a lay jury the importance of dose–response relationships and the meaning of risk assessment? Also, can a jury be made to understand that the term *carcinogen* is used loosely by the public—and even by some outstanding scientists? Much too often, an "experimental carcinogen" (i.e., one that induces a tumor in an experimental animal) is assumed, ipso facto, to be a "proven" human carcinogen. It may or may not be. The government dogma is that there is no threshold dose for a carcinogen; can the toxicologist help the jury understand that this is an edict and not an absolute scientific fact?

How, then, does a toxicologist react to the statement that a single fiber of asbestos penetrating a single cell starts an irreversible progress that inevitably leads to various cancers of the lung or other parts of the body? Many animal (or experimental) carcinogens are well known. Can the toxicologist explain the idea that animal carcinogens are suspected to be, but are not necessarily, human carcinogens? There are hundreds of animal (or experimental) carcinogens; there are only a very few proven human carcinogens.

Can a toxicologist present to a jury a logical explanation of the U.S. Environmental Protection Agency's (EPA) guidelines for declaring a chemical compound a carcinogen? These guidelines are based on information from epidemiology, results of a bioassay from two species of rodents, and some corroborative tests. How can the toxicologist keep the jury from being confused, when even the EPA does not always follow its own guidelines and relies instead on epidemiology alone to set standards for many regulated "carcinogens?" Is the toxicologist familiar with the World Health Organization's International Agency for Research on Cancer's (IARC) broad definition of a carcinogen—and that this definition does not state whether it applies to animals, or to humans, or to both?

All of these questions and problems may fall into the laps of toxicologists as members of this discipline are called into court more and more frequently. The toxicologist has the task of explaining to a judge and jury exactly what is toxicology, and why its quantitative aspects are so important.

The toxicologist faces a paradox. The modern science of toxicology is involved with not only what harm a chemical can do to a living system, but how much of that chemical it takes to cause that harm. This concept is well accepted. However, much of toxicology is not rigorous, and—unlike in chemistry, physics, and even engineering—there are no mathematical equations that really define toxicology. Even risk assessments, which do have formulas, still depend on subjective interpretation of biological phenomena. Risk assessment equations are legion. The same set of data, subject to different mathematical treatments of high to low dose extrapolation, can lead to risk estimates that differ by orders of magnitude.

No wonder, then, that results based on the same biological (toxicological) experiments can be interpreted differently by different toxicologists. Bias can enter into conclusions if there is an agenda other than pure science. It must be realized that politics, finances, and frame of mind can sway a toxicologist's conclusion.

Toxicology expertise is also needed in regulatory rule making. Experts are often called before legislative committees at local, state, or national levels. New uses for toxicologists are at trials for "whistle-blowers," and even for cases of scientific misconduct. Some states mandate that an expert be used in certain cases, especially if another expert is being sued for professional negligence. Toxicologists are also called upon to testify in arbitrations, administrative hearings, and sometimes negotiations.

Not many toxicologists have the experience to testify effectively; not all attorneys know how to deal with competent scientists, let alone those of a relatively new profession such as toxicology. Perhaps this can be said of other disciplines as well; members of other scientific disciplines may also find this book useful. Attorneys seem to be more familiar and therefore more at ease with members of the medical profession. At any rate, toxicologists as expert witnesses are presently in great demand, and too many toxicologists who are willing to be expert witnesses have no real experience with and are somewhat confused by the legal process.

This book, aimed at the toxicologist who intends to be useful as either the plaintiff's or defense's expert, was written to rectify this situation. Someone must take on the responsibility—either the attorney, the paralegal, or the toxicologist him- or herself—for the "care and feeding of the toxicologist as an expert witness" and provide the necessary hints so that the toxicologist can be the most effective witness possible. Someone must remind the testifying toxicologist that he or she is, in the main, a teacher, an explainer of complicated phenomena. In the courtroom, the toxicologist must think of the proverbial idea of teaching physics to poets.

In addition, both plaintiff and defense lawyers and their paralegals can profit from using this book, which is written from the viewpoint of an experienced toxicologist who is not a legal expert. This book can also be useful to other scientists, especially in related fields, because most situations described here have universal applications.

INTRODUCTION

Without a doubt, at the present time in the United States, toxic torts dominate the courts' attention. This relatively recent aspect of legal proceedings came to the foreground only in the 1980s. Toxic torts are all-inclusive; they relate to any exposure to some (noxious) agent that (will, can, may) result in an adverse effect on an individual person, a group of people, property of varying size, or the entire environment. As in other types of litigation, topics such as burden of proof and determining who is at fault must be considered.

A major problem for the testifying expert is that various states have different laws in regard to litigating these matters. At times the purpose of such litigation is not for monetary compensation but rather to require an industry or even a government agency to comply with environmental statutes.

This phenomenon has created a new role for both toxicologists and scientists from related disciplines. Such scientists are called upon to act as experts for attorneys who wish to present their cases in as strong and logical a manner as possible. Modern science and scientific concepts have become extremely complex; therefore an interpreter is needed to help a court come to a fair decision and a just conclusion about a case. This book, titled *The Toxicologist as Expert Witness* (which is essentially a treatise on "the care and feeding of the expert witness"), was written to help the scientist, especially the toxicologist, who is asked (or has volunteered) to be an expert witness. Although this book emphasizes the expert in the courtroom, many experts will never appear in court, but will be used to help resolutions of disputes settled out of court, or after arbitration. The expert, however, must always be prepared to appear in the courtroom.

For the scientist who has not had experience in court, this situation is like no other. To survive in the rough and tumble of the courtroom, the scientist must have a relatively strong ego and must be more than comfortable with his or her facts, conclusions, and opinions. Being an expert witness is not for the faint at heart! During the course of a trial, an expert may be challenged as to his or her veracity, integrity, morality (or similar words), or even emotional stability. Questions may be asked (or statements made) implying that the expert witness is a scientific "prostitute" whose testimony has been bought and paid for. Many opposing attorneys refer to the expert witness in pejorative terms like "hired guns." Even some members of the general public believe that expert witnesses will, as did Faust, sell their souls for a fee.

This book can be considered a "hint book"; it is meant to be just that. It contains hints for the expert witness (novice or experienced) about what to expect, what to do, and what not to do. This book is not a "handbook" in the technical sense. It does contain useful practical information; but with certain exceptions, it does not give details from actual cases or quotations from legal opinions. These are left to the attorney, who must explain to the expert the importance of any previous court's decision. The lawyer who reads this book may recognize the origin of some of these hints. This book emphasizes that the lawyer must have a continuous dialog with the expert witness. When the lawyer who hires the expert asks difficult questions, the expert should not feel that it reflects a lack of confidence in his or her qualifications or opinions.

Reviews of procedure at the most elementary levels are often indicated. Again, this need points out the importance of a continuous dialog between the attorney and the scientist-expert. The expert knows the science; the lawyer knows the law; neither is a perfect person; they must learn to work together. The expert witness must also learn much about the jury and the judge in a case—and not to get frustrated when a judge makes certain decisions regarding the admissibility of certain testimony. For, after all, who is really competent to decide what minimal acceptable science is?

This publication is not intended to be a scholarly treatise. Not every statement is followed by a citation, nor will footnotes appear quoting legal opinion. Only a very few critical precedent-setting cases are mentioned by name. The references at the end of the book are general ones that can help the expert become a better witness, but there are no special citations to these references. The attorney may call the attention of the expert to other useful publications that may be found in the local law library. One way an expert can help his or her attorney is to bring specific pertinent publications to the lawyer–expert conference. Wherever possible, photocopies of these scientific papers should be provided; the lawyer will appreciate this courtesy. The expert must not believe the attorney is devoid of all scientific information. There are many books written for lawyers on a variety of technical subjects, and some lawyers are very familiar with the relevant scientific literature.

The reader will find some repetition in different chapters in this book; this repetition is provided for emphasis and as a reminder of the importance of the topic.

To differentiate between the expert who will be expected to testify if a case goes to court and other experts in general, including the nontestifying expert, the capitalized "EXPERT" is used as the designation for the former, and the simple term "expert" is used for the latter. Likewise, the capitalized "ATTOR-NEY" refers to the engaging attorney, or the client attorney; the capitalized "LAWYER" is the attorney who represents the opposing party.

ACKNOWLEDGMENTS

I should like to acknowledge many attorneys who shall remain unnamed who, although successful in the courtroom, still did not know how to present a toxicologist to the court. This situation made me learn the hard way how to be an expert and effective witness, and thus to testify under less-than-ideal conditions.

There are a few attorneys, again unnamed, who did encourage me and teach me pointers so that I could be a more impressive testifying toxicologist; they gave me hints here and there about my conduct in the courtroom. In the main, however, most attorneys who have asked me to help in a case have assumed that I knew everything about testifying and needed no hints. How wrong they were. This book acknowledges both groups of attorneys.

My thanks to Mrs. Percy Noe, who cheerfully typed draft after draft of this book for me.

Chapter 1

What Is an Expert Witness?

In days gone by, an "expert" was defined as "an ordinary person with a brief-case at least 50 miles away from home." Our culture is too complicated for that type of humor now. There are two main types of witnesses in court cases. The first is the *lay*, or *fact*, witness (or *eyewitness*), who tells what he or she has personally seen and heard. In other words, the testimony is legally limited to what this witness has actually personally perceived. This witness, therefore, can relate firsthand knowledge of only certain limited facts. The fact witness cannot interpret or describe what others did, saw, or thought; nor can this witness express an opinion on the subject in the trial. The fact witness can tell the jury what he or she has experienced, not what he or she thinks.

In contrast, an *EXPERT* or *technical* witness, unlike the fact witness, can express an opinion within the scope of his or her experience, and also about facts or opinions that have been presented by others in previous testimony. There are boundaries to consider before a toxicologist is designated an EX-PERT; however, there is actually very little guidance on this issue. One caution: The EXPERT is not to be an advocate.

The EXPERT's testimony must:

- pertain to a subject whose technology is beyond common experience; this testimony must be of benefit to the "trier of fact"[1] by helping the trier of fact to determine the true facts or to understand complicated evidence;
- be based on material from admissible evidence of a type that an expert may reasonably rely on to form an opinion;
- be made by someone who has special knowledge, experience, education, and skill to qualify as an expert; and
- in a sense, be limited to a specific area of knowledge.

The EXPERT may discuss the opinion of another expert (even if that opinion is not admissible in evidence; here a fine line must be drawn and the ATTORNEY must give guidance) but cannot use only the conclusions of other scientists. Also, circumstantial evidence can be used for an opinion, but, to avoid conflicts, the EXPERT must be careful to establish the foundation for such an opinion.

It is permissible for an EXPERT to give an opinion on "hearsay" testimony,[2] which normally is excluded from court hearings. This hearsay testimony must be of a type usually relied upon by other experts in the field in which this EXPERT is testifying. There is thus some leeway for the EXPERT to express an opinion on the case. Unpublished information may, in some cases, be relied upon by the EXPERT. The courts are troubled, however, by what is called "hearsay in disguise." There have been different conclusions when one EXPERT relies on the opinion of another expert who will not testify. The difficulty is whether the court thinks the EXPERT has actually relied on the opinion of the other expert or whether the EXPERT affirms that the other expert agrees with the testifying EXPERT's opinion—in other words, "consistent with. . . ." A major problem occurs when the EXPERT includes in his or her opinion information from a conversation with another expert.

In the long run, the EXPERT must demonstrate the validity of his or her analysis of the facts and the conclusions drawn from these facts. In some cases, an EXPERT may testify that the discussion or even the opinion he or she gives, although counter to mainstream science, is derived from the real facts. The complication is that some theories are sound, whereas others are "junk"[3] science. It is often difficult for a lay group like a jury to distinguish between

[1]The "trier of fact" is the jury in a jury trial, or the judge if a jury trial is waived.
[2]Hearsay testimony is testimony about out-of-court statements made by a third party offered as truth.
[3]A document titled *Report of the Tort Policy Working Group*, published by the U.S. Attorney General's Office in 1984, approached the problem of junk science. The report noted:

Another way in which causation is undermined—also an increasing serious problem in toxic tort cases—is the reliance by judges and juries on noncredible scientific or medical testimony, studies or opinions. It has become all too common for "experts" or "studies" on the fringes or even well beyond the outer parameters of mainstream scientific or medical views to be presented to juries as valid evidence from which conclusions may be drawn. The use of such invalid scientific evidence (commonly referred to as "junk science") has resulted in finding of causation which cannot be justified or understood from the standpoint of current state of credible scientific and medical knowledge.

different conclusions presented by opposing expert witnesses. The jury cannot necessarily differentiate between the scientist with credentials related to the topic before the court and the scientist—who may also have impressive credentials, not necessarily in the same discipline—who presents an unconventional interpretation of biomedical data. Not all unconventional hypotheses, however, are ipso facto wrong.

Unfortunately, at present, there are a number of scientists (or even lay people) without formal training or experience to qualify as toxicologists who are nonetheless being represented as experts in toxicology. A few approach the witness stand with an air of authority and then present theories and conclusions contrary to accepted dogma. In many cases junk science is expounded. The result is a battle of the experts.

The EXPERT, more than the court, should be able to explain some basis of distinguishing real from junk science. One can conclude that a theory is junk science if the pet hypothesis cannot be repeated and verified.

The EXPERT should determine if the hypothesis has been published in a peer-reviewed journal. (The EXPERT must explain peer review to the jury.) A peer-reviewed article has the most likely chance of having no substantial flaws in methodology, but this is not an absolute! The technique used must not be too prone to error, and the original Frye Rule (see below) must still be considered: Does the hypothesis have widespread acceptance? This latter, however, is not the sole criterion for acceptance as good versus junk science.

The toxicologist must recognize that science is dynamic; ideas can change as one builds to a greater truth. In contrast, the law must resolve disputes in a short finite period of time and in a final manner. Thus, it is possible that much science will be "decided" by the legal system and not by the body of science!

GUIDING RULES

The standards to be considered for the testimony of a scientist originally came from two main sources, the Frye Rule (sometimes referred to as the Kelly-Frye test) and the Federal Rules of Evidence (FRE) enacted on June 1, 1995. These rules pertain to federal courts, but their use is widespread in state courts.

About seventy years ago, in *Frye v. United States*, an expert presented a novel physiological test that used the change in systolic blood pressure to detect if a witness was telling the truth or lying. The presiding judge refused to admit evidence based upon this physiological test because there was no real agreement among knowledgeable scientists on the value of its technique. In a sense, the Frye Rule dealt with the question of which evidence can be excluded by a presiding judge—that is, evidence not derived from normal scientific techniques. As a result, judges have the prerogative to rule out certain novel approaches or unpopular scientific opinions. Thus, the deduction a scientist makes must come from science that is sufficiently established and has gained general acceptance in its field.

Besides the Frye Rule, there are a number of rules in the FRE with which an EXPERT should be acquainted to make it easier for him or her to give an opinion. The ATTORNEY should brief the EXPERT on these rules. For those EXPERTS who spend a fair amount of time in a courtroom, it may be wise to obtain the entire publication.

Important Federal Rules

Rule 104A requires a "preliminary assessment of whether the reasoning and methodology can be applied to the facts of the case." The court should (but does not have to) consider whether the proposed scientific theory has been tested, and whether the scientific idea has been subjected to peer review and publication. Rule 402 notes that only relevant evidence is admissible; nonrelevant evidence is not.

Rule 702 provides the reasoning for appointing an EXPERT and focuses on principles and methodology, not on the conclusions they generate. This rule is very flexible. In short, it states that judges have the authority to limit admissible evidence if it will cause confusion or unfairly prejudice the court. There are no exact guidelines on how to do so; however, science may not matter if a jury finds sufficient evidence of cause in a legal sense. This rule also appears to permit a judge to screen out some expert testimony before a jury can hear it. Rule 702 also states that the EXPERT is to help the trier of fact understand the technical aspects of a case.

> If scientific, technical or other specialized knowledge will assist the trier of fact to understand the evidence or to determine a fact in issue, a witness qualified as an expert by knowledge, skill, experience, training or education, may testify thereto in the form of an advisory opinion or otherwise.

Rule 703 gives the basis for an expert opinion, in a vague fashion: The opinion must be "of a type reasonably relied upon by experts in the particular field." There have been different interpretations of Rule 703. The question revolves on whether the court can independently assess the reasonableness of a scientist's reliance on data or facts. Some trial judges believe they can determine what is unreasonable and thus reject an EXPERT's testimony. Some courts have permitted an expert opinion where there is no "general acceptance."

The EXPERT should expect that the ATTORNEY is familiar with the FRE; the EXPERT needs the ATTORNEY's guidance on what type of information is acceptable to a court. This is not to say, however, that the ATTORNEY should tell the EXPERT what to say. At all times, the EXPERT must tell the truth.

Recent Supreme Court Rulings

The above rules have been somewhat modified by the recent Supreme Court decision relating to *Daubert v. Merrell Dow Pharmaceuticals, Inc.* (U.S. 951

F.2D 1128 (9th Cir 1991) cert. granted 113S, Sup. Ct. 320 (1992)), in which the court ruled that there is a two-part test for the admissibility of expert testimony. First, the expert's testimony must reflect "scientific knowledge" and whether the findings are "derived from the scientific method" and amount to "good science." Second, the court must ensure that the proposed testimony is "relevant to the task at hand" and that it logically advances a material aspect of the proposing party's case. This second part of the test is called the "fit" requirement. The expert testimony must "fit" by applying accepted science to the facts of the case.

From a toxicologist's point of view, several comments can be made about this recent Supreme Court decision. Rules are now more liberal in admitting (or even excluding) expert testimony. Justice Harry Blackmun made statements that were critical of the more narrow Frye Rule in the majority opinion that should make toxicologists reflect on their pending testimony. He noted, "There are important differences between the quest for truth in the courtroom and the quest for truth in the laboratory" and that "general acceptance" is not a precondition to the admissibility of scientific evidence under FRE—especially Rule 702.

If scientific, technical, or other specialized knowledge will assist the trier of fact to understand the evidence or to determine a fact in issue, an expert *may testify thereto*.

The ATTORNEY should explain why the Frye Rule, or the Frye Test (evidence must be accepted by the scientific community), was too rigid for the Supreme Court and why the FRE are more flexible. However, there are still stringent restrictions as to what evidence can be accepted by the court. The trial judge must decide if the EXPERT's opinion is truly scientific and can assist the jury while they determine the facts as related to the scientific issues. The judge must also decide if the scientific evidence is reliable. Acceptance by the scientific community is not now the major criterion. The judge must decide if the evidence will assist the jury in deliberation; on the other hand, the judge may actually rule out good scientific evidence if, as the judge sees it, the evidence will mislead or prejudice the jury. Attorneys often argue about the wisdom of giving the judges such authority; it is now up to the judge's discretion to determine if novel, but credible, theories will be kept away from a jury.

At this writing, there may be other court decisions pending relative to the *Daubert* case. Many states are interpreting the *Daubert* decision differently, and many states are making new laws that will affect the nature of the testimony an EXPERT may give. In the future, these new laws may also be challenged in the Supreme Court. Also, the EXPERT and ATTORNEY must be aware that the present Congress is altering the laws regarding product liability. These new laws may also be challenged in a higher court.

Judges As "Gatekeepers"

Under Rule 702, Justice Blackmun intended for trial judges to act as "gatekeepers." With this power, a judge can decide what evidence can be presented to, and what information must be withheld from, a jury. In the *Daubert* majority opinion, Chief Justice William Rehnquist and Associate Justice John Paul Stevens warned that judges must become "amateur scientists." Federal judges must possess the capacity to decide "whether the reasoning or methodology underlying the testimony is scientifically valued . . . and can be applied to the case."

As gatekeeper, a judge has the responsibility to determine whether the testimony is on sound scientific principles and if "any and all testimony or evidence admitted is not only relevant, but reliable." This power can lead to a judge excluding unorthodox but relevant testimony.

The *Daubert* case does not permit a judge to decide if there is sufficient evidence for an expert to come to a conclusion.

In 1994, the U.S. Court of Appeals for the Third Circuit upheld the judge's role as gatekeeper to make an independent assessment of the reliability of the materials used by an expert in coming to a conclusion. The judge can conduct an independent evaluation of the reasonableness, as outlined in Rule 703.

Judges under Rule 702 can decide not only on an expert witness's qualifications, but also on his or her methodology and scientific principles, as well as conclusions! This rule permits a judge to accept one expert's opinion as being superior to that of the opposing expert. The toxicologist must be aware that if a judge decides that any step in an expert's analysis is unreliable, that expert's testimony becomes inadmissible!

Judges have other powers besides acting as gatekeepers. A judge can limit the number of experts who can be called to testify by either the ATTORNEY or LAWYER.

WHAT DOES IT TAKE?

In light of the recent Supreme Court decision and the attempts to clarify the judge's gatekeeping role by the Third Circuit Court of Appeals, it is now more important than ever for the toxicologist as an expert witness to be fully qualified as a member in good standing of the relevant profession. Membership in a toxicology association (Society of Toxicology, American College of Toxicology, etc.) is of paramount importance.

The EXPERT should also, if possible, be designated as diplomate (not diplomat!) in either of the two accrediting agencies, the American Board of Toxicology (ABT) or the Academy of Toxicological Sciences (ATS). A physician may have an MD or OD degree and also be a board-certified medical specialist in internal medicine, surgery, or some other specialty. The general public is familiar with this system. In contrast, the designation of board-certified toxicologist is practically unknown to the majority of professionals, including attorneys and judges.

The use of the acronyms DABT and FATS (Diplomate of the American Board of Toxicology or Fellow of the Academy of Toxicological Sciences) denoting diplomate status is meaningful for those in the toxicology profession, but meaningless for the vast majority of the public, including many attorneys. It is incumbent on the toxicologist who is a diplomate of either of the two accrediting agencies to be aware of the significance of accreditation and convey this to the jury and to the LAWYER. (It is assumed that the ATTORNEY will have been so advised.)

To become a diplomate of either of the two boards, a candidate must fill out a detailed questionnaire and submit it with a fee to: The Academy of Toxicological Sciences, 9200 Leesburg Pike, Vienna, VA 22182; or to The American Board of Toxicology, P.O. Box 30054, Raleigh, NC 27622-0054.

The ATS requires the candidate to have proven ability, experience, and fundamental competence in toxicology. The three classes of qualifications for certification as a FATS are Education and Training, Professional Experience, and Demonstration of Scientific Judgment and Recognition. Each division within a class is assigned points by the members of the ATS board of directors after they have reviewed the credentials submitted by a candidate. If there is a conflict, or even a potential conflict, a board member excuses him- or herself. Each fellow must be recertified after a five-year period. As is to be expected, only toxicologists with years of experience apply for the FATS.

The requirements to become a DABT are different; they include the combination of a degree and a number of years of experience, depending on the level of the degree. The degree should be in toxicology or a related field. A written examination is required, which covers three fields: toxicology of agents (specific chemicals such as metals, solvents, etc.); special toxicology (biological effects on systems); and general principles and applied toxicology. The candidate must pass all three parts within a two-year period. Recertification is required every five years.

Above all, an EXPERT must be of good character, honest, and committed to good science. Truth is the most important ingredient in the EXPERT's armamentarium. The EXPERT must also be accessible to the ATTORNEY who hires the EXPERT. If the EXPERT is too busy, the ATTORNEY should know early on. It goes without saying that the EXPERT must be an expert in communication skills as well as the science of the case.

The qualifications of an expert witness include the following:

1   The EXPERT must have a combination of special knowledge, skill, experience, training, and education to qualify as an expert on the *subject in dispute*. Often, an expert with practical experience is more acceptable to jurors, and thus more favorably received by the court, than one who deals only in the realm of academic theoretical evaluation. A question presently in dispute is whether the expert must have some publications in a refereed journal.

2   Testimony must pertain to a subject that is sufficiently beyond common experience. The information given by the EXPERT must be of benefit to the trier of fact, if it is assumed that the latter should generally not be expected to have this knowledge. It is also expected that a reasonably educated jury should not have this specific technical knowledge.

3 Testimony must be based on material of a type that an expert may reasonably rely on to form an opinion.

An EXPERT is not needed to state facts that anyone can attest to. For example, the EXPERT need not make a statement that "a dark liquid leaked from the corroded barrel, and the fumes made my eyes tear," or "the spilled liquid smelled like rotten eggs."

Some ATTORNEYS do, however, have EXPERTS quote the facts of a case to the jury, because these ATTORNEYS believe that such testimony impresses a jury.

ABOUT EXPERT WITNESSES

An expert in a case is only an EXPERT if so declared by the presiding judge. The judge may also declare what limitations are imposed on the testimony of an EXPERT.

The success of an EXPERT in court also depends upon the attention given to all facets of the case, to its details, and especially to his or her preparation. A good EXPERT is basically an excellent teacher. However, an EXPERT never wins or loses a case; the EXPERT merely assists the ATTORNEY who does win or lose.

Some EXPERTS use too many technical terms, which may confuse jury members or impress them. In too many cases, the juries cannot deal with the facts in the case without the opinion of an EXPERT. Many courts have given great scrutiny to the qualifications of the EXPERT, questioning if he or she is really an expert in the area of concern. Some judges have warned juries about the abuse of expert testimony.

The name(s) of the EXPERT(S) must be revealed to the LAWYER in civil cases, but not necessarily in criminal cases. Likewise, depositions may be taken by the opposing LAWYER in civil cases, but not always in criminal cases. The advice of the ATTORNEY is recommended for understanding the rules in a particular state. In rare cases where one expert is used to impeach another, it may not be necessary to reveal that this new expert will be used. For example: A toxicologist may be brought in to explain to the jury that the local high school biology teacher is not accepted as an expert on toxicology by the profession of toxicologists.

The prospective EXPERT should realize that some lawyers will try various means to keep an opposing expert out of court. There may be attempts to prevent the opposite side from hiring the EXPERT. One way to keep an expert from helping the opposition is to sign him or her up as a consultant, give him or her very little work to do, but give him or her confidential information. Ethically, the expert with this information cannot discuss the case with others and is therefore never available for the opposite side. Another tactic is to engage an expert as an EXPERT and have a written contract, but then never use him or her. In either case, the expert is safely removed from action. If this ever happens to a potential EXPERT, that person should at least try to negotiate a higher fee.

The toxicologist must be protected in the initial contact by telling the ATTORNEY who is interested in engaging him or her as an EXPERT that this is a preliminary interview, and only general terms can be discussed; however, the ATTORNEY may describe an outline of the case, provided no privileged or confidential information is included. This meeting should be followed up by writing stating clearly that no confidential information was received; the toxicologist must be careful not to get into a conflict of interest.

If the other side calls, it is important for the potential EXPERT to make it clear that he or she has already been contacted by an opposing attorney. The decision to accept or not to accept an assignment is a personal choice. But the potential EXPERT should *get it all in writing*.

It cannot be overemphasized that the EXPERT in court is not an advocate. It is the ATTORNEY who is the advocate for his or her client and must try to win the trial by any legal means. The ATTORNEY will try to seek a favorable verdict, and will not be concerned with a balanced verdict.

SPECIAL CASES

Most attorneys are more comfortable using engineers or members of the medical profession as expert witnesses. These professions are well known and characterized. Normally, members of a jury are acquainted with one who calls him- or herself an engineer, regardless of the type of engineer, or a doctor, again regardless of specialty. Thus, introducing to the judge a member of either of these two professions as a potential expert witness presents no problem, nor any question to the jury. However, a special case presents itself when the jury first hears that the expert being qualified is a *toxicologist*.

The Nontestifying Toxicologist

In general, a toxicologist need not be considered different from any other scientific or technical witness, such as a chemist or physiologist. Once the toxicologist explains to the jury what toxicology is all about, and how this discipline differs from pharmacology or chemistry, there should not be a problem in the courtroom. The jury will understand what a toxicologist does—and that the toxicologist does not only deal with poisons!

Despite the emphasis on the testifying EXPERT, there is another important class of expert: the nontestifying expert, a consultant who should be as knowledgeable as the EXPERT. This expert can also play a crucial role in litigation. The advice given by the nontestifying expert to the ATTORNEY is privileged, not subject to discovery—provided all written reports, notes, comments, and invoices are headed "Privileged and Confidential—Prepared at the Request of Counsel in Anticipation of Litigation." These notes are the ATTORNEY's work product. Needless to say, the privilege is lost if any of these work products are given to anyone other than the ATTORNEY.

Many tasks noted in this book as belonging to the EXPERT can be relegated to the nontestifying expert. Included are the tasks of assisting the ATTORNEY with questions to ask the opposing expert during the deposition and framing technical questions to ask prospective jurors. Hints can be given to the ATTORNEY about the type of juror who can understand the nature of the EXPERT's testimony; it is desirable to get at least one juror who will understand the science of the case.

Although they are not toxicologists per se, special recognition must be given to the forensic experts who are highly trained technical experts.

Women as Expert Witnesses

None of the "how to" books on the expert witness appear to be aware of the special problems a woman toxicologist may have on the witness stand; the general references simply use a unisex approach. Women as expert witnesses have complained many times about their treatment on the stand. Many women believe they are more subject to verbal abuse. For instance, many women believe that the LAWYER gives more credence to a male's testimony than theirs. Women experts, more than their male counterparts, seem to be the subject of personal questions about their home life, their marital status, their motherly duties, their living conditions, and their socioeconomic status. Some questions may even touch on the sex life of a female EXPERT. These same questions are very seldom asked of a male EXPERT; too often the ATTORNEY does not brief the woman EXPERT on how to deal with them.

One woman EXPERT, while giving her testimony, looked at the first row of the court spectators and suddenly saw the face of the man from whom she had been divorced for many years. Thus, a unique form of harassment was employed! The LAWYER had actually paid the ex-husband to fly to the trial and sit in the front row to disconcert the EXPERT.

ETHICAL CONSIDERATIONS

The EXPERT must at all times be aware that there is an obligation to at least three taskmasters. Never should any one of these obligations override the necessity of being completely ethical in all dealings with other professionals, be they toxicologists or members of the legal profession.

First, the ATTORNEY must receive the EXPERT's complete loyalty. At no time can the EXPERT be in professional contact with the opposing side. If a contact is made by a LAWYER, the ATTORNEY must be notified at once.

The second obligation is to the profession. An unprofessional toxicologist who disregards the code of ethics of a toxicology organization can cause that organization to lose status and credibility in the eyes of the public. It is well known that many lay persons are already suspicious of scientists in general. One unethical member tars the entire membership.

The Society of Toxicology adopted a standard code of ethics in 1985. The code is:

Preamble

The Society of Toxicology is dedicated to developing knowledge for the improvement of the health and safety of living beings and the protection of the environment.

In obtaining this objective each Member must maintain high ethical standards and, to this purpose, this code requires a personal commitment.

Code of Ethics

I, as a member shall

Strive to conduct my work and myself with objectivity and integrity.

Hold as inviolate that credible science is fundamental to all toxicological research.

Seek to communicate information concerning health, safety, and toxicity in a timely and responsible manner, with due regard for the significance and credibility of the available data.

Present my scientific statements or endorsements with full disclosure of whether or not factual supportive data are available.

Abstain from professional judgments influenced by conflict of interest and, insofar as possible, avoid situations that imply a conflict of interest.

Observe the spirit as well as the letter of law, regulation and ethical standards with regard to the welfare of humans and animals involved in my experimental procedures.

Practice high standards of occupational health and safety for the benefit of my co-workers and other personnel.

This code of ethics does not address the testifying EXPERT specifically, but it can certainly be considered applicable to the situation.

The third and most important taskmaster for the EXPERT is him- or herself. A code of ethics is not needed to remind the EXPERT that he or she must be open and careful that the testimony presented to the court is intellectually honest. At all times, the EXPERT must speak the complete truth; half or partial truths are not tolerable. The EXPERT must be careful never to bend the truth even slightly to please a colleague or the ATTORNEY. On the other hand, an honest mistake is not to be considered unethical.

The specific ethical violations that must be avoided include: giving false information, fabricating data from an experiment not done, ignoring available data, accepting an assignment beyond one's competence, and reaching a conclusion before all research is completed. A question of ethics can arise if the EXPERT renders an opinion in one case and then gives a completely opposite opinion in another, similar case.

A question of ethics can also arise if an ATTORNEY engages an EXPERT to testify as a plaintiff's witness in one case and at the same time as a defense witness in another, similar case. Another question can arise if an EXPERT testifies in one case against a LAWYER, but at the same time is an EXPERT for the same LAWYER in a different case.

In the future, the toxicologist will have to interact with the bioethicist. New laws will have to be written to guarantee the privacy of genetic information. As the nature of human genetics is unveiled, people will be diagnosed with, for example, an oncogene. Can such people be protected against genetic discrimination? In the future, will the court see cases of this nature?

Chapter 2

So You Want to Be an Expert

A toxicologist new to the field of testifying in toxic tort cases must decide if he or she really wants to subject him- or herself to the ordeal of the rough and tumble of the courtroom proceedings. The toxicologist should do some careful and "gut-level" thinking about the realities of a courtroom battle, because the toxicologist as an EXPERT will have to stand up to potentially abusive attacks. The outcome of a trial is more often based on the toxicologist's testimony than that of any other witness, factual or expert.

The EXPERT must be objective, but not disinterested. The EXPERT must be somewhat involved, but not an advocate. There is a fine distinction here. It is possible that the EXPERT's views may change somewhat as he or she learns more about the facts of a case or the pertinent literature, but the EXPERT must never alter his or her thinking or written opinion just to please the ATTORNEY.

WHAT ARE YOUR QUALIFICATIONS?

In general, an EXPERT has sufficient knowledge of the facts of a case to evaluate them, and this knowledge permits an opinion. Most often, the question boils down to the following: "Did the substance to which a party was exposed *cause* the specific injury claimed?"

There are real and there are quasi-knowledgeable experts; there are well-intentioned scientists who are not qualified in a particular field. Also available are fakes, phonies, and frauds who, for a fee, or because they firmly believe that they alone can be right, are willing to testify and to give opinions. The qualifications of the real EXPERT therefore become critical to enabling the jury to understand and believe his or her scientific testimony.

What, then, are your qualifications that give you a right to have an opinion on a case? Can you present to a jury at least a minimum of:

Education

What degree(s) do you have? From what school or college? What year was that degree given? What was your major subject; what were your minors?

Note: Until recently, most universities had no toxicology department per se. Degrees in toxicology were given by pharmacology departments in both medical and pharmacy schools. Some graduate schools offered a toxicology emphasis in a more traditional department.

Note: Because a PhD in toxicology is a relatively recent phenomenon, a number of toxicologists came to the field from chemistry, biochemistry, physiology, pathology, and the like. If you are one of these people, it is of utmost importance to explain to the jury why a "physiologist" is appearing in court as a "toxicologist."

Experience

Teaching   Have you taught some phase of toxicology? What was the nature of your teaching? Did you teach a specific course in toxicology? Were you in a toxicology department, or at least in a toxicology program? Did you teach undergraduates or graduates, or both?

Practical Experience   What industrial experience do you have? How many years? What is the relationship between toxicology and your work?

Research

Have you actually done toxicological research, or worked in a similar field? If the latter, how do you relate your research project to toxicology? How many years of experience do you have in the various fields related to toxicology? Have you conducted any study or experiment(s) related to this specific court case? If not, have you been associated with a project that can be related to this case?

Publications

What have you published in toxicology? How many publications? Have you published any papers specifically related to the subject of this court case? What are the references? (If necessary, you must explain to a jury the difference between refereed journals and nonrefereed journals. This aspect of qualifications will become more and more important as time goes on.)

Professional Organizations

Do you belong to a professional society that requires presenting credentials to a membership committee? Are you a member of the American College of Toxicology (ACT) or the Society of Toxicology (SOT)? (If necessary, explain to the jury the difference between being a member of a scientific organization like the American Chemical Society (ACS) or the American Association for the Advancement of Science (AAAS) and qualifying as a member in ACT or SOT. Any chemist with minimal qualifications can join and pay dues to the ACS; and the AAAS accepts any interested person. In these two toxicology organizations, a candidate's qualifications must be screened by a membership committee before he or she can be accepted.)

Honors

Are you board-certified in toxicology? Are you a diplomate of the ABT, having successfully passed the required tests; or are you a fellow of the ATS, having satisfied its board of directors of your extensive background in toxicology? Are you a fellow of any scientific organization? (If necessary, explain to the jury the meaning of being designated a fellow.) What other honors have been bestowed on you?

WHAT MAKES YOU UNCOMFORTABLE?

Very early in the relationship between the ATTORNEY and the EXPERT, the discussion should include areas of science or personal problems that are uncomfortable for the EXPERT. Actually, the ATTORNEY should bring this matter up at the first meeting or soon thereafter.

All topics should be aired. Do you have a problem with the fee? Will you hesitate to tell the jury what reimbursements are expected? This can be an awkward subject for an EXPERT, who will be aware that the jurors receive less than $10.00 per day and are reimbursed for mileage for only one way.

Will you have a problem identifying the ultimate client? Naturally, the ATTORNEY is visible, but what if the ultimate client is very unpopular, for example a drug lord or a convicted felon?

Do you have a problem with the case about to be tried? Are you convinced that the chemical in question caused the alleged pathology, even though you have been hired as a defense EXPERT, or convinced that it is not the cause, even though you have been hired as a plaintiff's EXPERT?

Is there a real fear that you will not make a good witness on the stand?

Do you have a skeleton in the closet? Is there anything in your academic record that can be questioned?

In what other types of cases, especially unpopular ones, have you testified? Will testifying on a drug case, an alcohol case, a tobacco case, a murder case redound in unfavorable reactions from your peers?

Hint: Early on, the EXPERT must tell the ATTORNEY about any real or potential skeletons in the closet.

WILL YOU ACCEPT SUGGESTIONS?

The EXPERT must be aware at all times what his or her function is relative to the case under consideration. An ATTORNEY may hint at, or openly suggest, the idea of an EXPERT's becoming an advocate. This is never the function of the EXPERT, and it is essential for the EXPERT to avoid being placed in an untenable position. Of course, because the ATTORNEY is paying the fee of the EXPERT, the ATTORNEY expects that the EXPERT act as a positive force on the witness stand.

Often an ATTORNEY tries to strengthen his or her case by putting words in an EXPERT's mouth. This should be resisted. Sometimes an ATTORNEY wishes to hear how an EXPERT will answer certain questions. This is to help the ATTORNEY understand the thinking process of the EXPERT. There should be no problem with this. The EXPERT must listen with a "third ear" to screen out material given to the EXPERT by the ATTORNEY that is irrelevant to the present case.

Your ATTORNEY will always want you to use a vocabulary that can be understood by a jury. The ATTORNEY can give many hints on how to express ideas and how to explain complicated facts. Will you accept hints? Can you use simple words and avoid jargon and still stay within acceptable science? The following examples offering dual explanations for the same phenomena should be useful in your consideration of situations relevant to the case:

1 A crucial fact in a trial is how visible an object is at twilight.
   a Jargon: The light meter reading near the object was so many units of light.
   b Lay language: It was light enough to read a newspaper under the street light.
2 How the body deals with a pollutant is an important fact in a trial.
   a Jargon: Foreign bodies are biotransformed by hepatic oxygenase P-450 isoenzymes.
   b Lay language: Toxic materials can be detoxified by the liver, by a process similar to how food is digested (or metabolized).
3 A "slow" metabolizer is at greater risk than a "fast" metabolizer for side effects of a drug in question.

   a Jargon: The kinetics of biotransformation and hence excretion are retarded.

   b Lay language: For some people, the body neutralizes or inactivates a drug so slowly that the drug remains in the body longer.

4 A compound in question is an isomer of a known toxic compound.

   a Jargon: Because the compound of concern here is an isomer of a known toxic compound, then by QSR, I conclude it is equally toxic.

   b Lay language: The compound in question is so similar chemically to a known toxic compound that a reasonable estimate is that this compound is also toxic.

5 The amount of toxic material that the victim was exposed to could not be more than . . .

   a Jargon: No more than 50 g of material was involved.

   b Lay language: The person was exposed to less than a half teaspoon, or two ounces, of the chemical.

Note: Lay audiences understand teaspoonful, half a tablespoon, and eight-ounce glass, but do not really relate to the metric system of milligrams, milliliters, and the like.

In other words, avoid technical language or the jargon of the discipline; use words that a high school graduate can understand. A trial is no place to show off.

If there will be more than one EXPERT used by your ATTORNEY, be sure that you, a paralegal, or the ATTORNEY coordinates the testimony. The testimony of each EXPERT must be consistent and, by all means, supportive if at all possible.

The opposing LAWYER may try to use one of the ATTORNEY's EXPERTS to invalidate or impeach the testimony of the ATTORNEY's other EXPERT. Naturally, the LAWYER will attempt to have his or her own EXPERT(S) nullify the opinions of all of the ATTORNEY's EXPERTS.

THE "IN-HOUSE" EXPERT

Prior to using an "in-house" toxicologist to testify, an industry lawyer must be consulted to check to see if the employment contract of that toxicologist permits him or her to testify in a court case. There are many advantages as well as disadvantages to using an in-house EXPERT to testify for either side.

The advantages are that this expert:

- cannot be considered a "hired gun,"
- knows the product,
- knows the intimate details of the manufacturing of the product,
- can help the ATTORNEY become acquainted with the industry environment, and
- knows the history of the toxicological testing.

Disadvantages to using the in-house expert include:

• The jury can be told that the in-house EXPERT must testify to keep his or her job;
• the LAWYER, on cross-examination, can allude to the pressure on the in-house EXPERT to testify, regardless of the facts;
• the EXPERT can give away trade secrets under cross-examination; and
• the EXPERT can be too critical of the company's product and thus adversely affect sales.

There is a catch-22 situation regarding whether an in-house EXPERT is used. The LAWYER can ask, "Are you reluctant to use an outside EXPERT who may find out too much about your product?" By the same token, an opposite stance can be taken when an in-house EXPERT is not used: The LAWYER can say, "Why did you use an outside expert—Don't you have anyone on your staff good enough?"

The implication is always that, although the in-house EXPERT is under oath, the company expects him or her to be willing to commit perjury. Perhaps the wisest strategy in any case is to use both an in-house EXPERT and an outside EXPERT, who can support the testimony of the in-house EXPERT.

THE COURT-APPOINTED EXPERT

Under certain circumstances, but rather infrequently, the court may appoint its own EXPERT. (This is permitted under Rule 706—and other rules—of the FRE.) Often the need for such an EXPERT is not recognized by the court. A judge has the authority to select specialists such as translators, speech handicap assistants, and the like; thus, it is logical for a judge to appoint a toxicologist if necessary, as well. Many judges will not find it difficult to find a qualified toxicology EXPERT.

The opposing parties may not be in favor of this strategy, and they may indeed be strongly opposed. If this is the case, they will not make suggestions as to who should be appointed as the EXPERT, nor participate in any way in the appointment. Sometimes, however, this special EXPERT is selected with the consent of both parties. Once designated, the EXPERT must be notified in writing, and his or her specific duties must be spelled out. The court-appointed EXPERT can greatly influence the outcome of litigation and at times facilitate settlement before a case goes to trial. The court-appointed expert can also be most helpful to the judge in pretrial hearings to help screen scientific testimony.

The jury looks on the court-appointed EXPERT as a truly neutral expert, who has much knowledge in the field in question and no regard for the interests of either party to the litigation. This EXPERT can break an evidence stalemate.

Prior to 1983, juries were not always told about such special appointments; juries are now made aware of them. Naturally, the court-appointed EXPERT is subject to cross-examination by attorneys from both sides. Compensation for the court-appointed EXPERT can be a problem, because the amount can be determined by the county in which the court resides. This amount can range from the amount given to a jury member to the usual fee charged by the EXPERT. In about 50% of the cases, the fee is set by the court. In civil cases both parties can be made to contribute to the fee; in criminal cases the state alone pays. When insufficient funds are available, the best qualified potential experts may not wish to get involved. Such a situation should be a rarity.

MARKETING YOURSELF

Before advertising yourself as an expert, you should prepare a short resume of your qualifications and keep it up-to-date. Your experience in testifying, if any, should be clearly stated. The resume should be printed in such a manner as to catch someone's eye. Your resume should also have a few notes, such as statements that you can speak well and can translate complicated scientific words into clear lay language.

Seldom is a toxicologist asked to be an EXPERT out of the blue. If you really are interested in being an EXPERT, it is necessary to let the law firms know that you exist. There are a number of ways to become known. For one, you should contact the local bar association and ask the librarian for suggestions about how attorneys can learn about you. There is an American Bar Association (ABA)–AAAS cooperative project. The prospective EXPERT witness should try to keep up on the progress of this joint project.

Let your toxicologist colleagues know you are available to be an EXPERT witness. It is wise to attend a "how-to" conference or workshop. Often in such conferences there is a session on getting started.

There are a number of reference services that have lists of experts to suggest to attorneys. (You pay a fee, of course, to be listed.) You may wish to call a local attorney who uses experts and inquire about which scientific reference service he or she uses. At the same time, let the attorney know you are available.

As a shot in the dark, you can mail a copy of your resume to some large law firms in your area. Almost every large law firm is interested in obtaining the names of new potential witnesses.

Most cities have the equivalent of a *Daily Law Journal*; there is also a *National Law Journal*. The librarian at the local bar association can give you the names and addresses of these publications. An ad in one of these newspapers catering to lawyers may be useful. It is best to obtain a copy of the journal to see who else advertises his or her services, and in what format.

Professional organizations may also provide opportunities. The ACS has a "Chemistry and Law" division. The SOT has a "Round Table of Consultants." Joining these and other scientific organizations can be helpful in furthering your goal to become an expert.

As mentioned, there are specific organizations that, for a fee, list available experts. Examples of helpful publications include (but are not limited to):

- the *Legal Expert Pages* from San Diego, California;
- the Northern California register of *Experts and Consultants*, San Francisco, California;
- the ASTM *Directory of Scientific & Technical Consultants and Expert Witnesses*, Philadelphia, Pennsylvania;
- *Society of Testifying Experts*, LRP Publications, Alexandria, Virginia; and
- *Lawyers Desk Reference*, Detroit, Michigan.

Other organizations to contact:

- Technical Advisory Service for Attorneys, Phoenix, Arizona;
- Expert Witness Network, Washington, DC;
- National Forensic Center, New Jersey;
- Round Table of Consultants (SOT members only), Santa Fe, New Mexico;
- Texas Lawyer (Expert Witness Department), Dallas, Texas; and
- Daily Journal Corporation, Los Angeles, California.

The local law librarian can give you the latest addresses of these organizations.

Seminars for the experienced and novice expert are given quite often all over the country (see *The Testifying Expert*, LRP Publications). Notices of these meetings are often posted in law libraries. For some, attendance fees are very expensive.

Your publications on both technical and nontechnical topics will find their way into some database or other. Letters to newspapers and journals on quasi-technical articles will also keep your name in public.

Finally, the Internet is a relatively new source of information. Many lawyers are listed, along with their addresses. Also, it should be possible to list yourself and your strengths.

Chapter 3

The Attorney–Expert Relationship

The ATTORNEY–EXPERT relationship starts after the ATTORNEY contacts the EXPERT by means of a letter, or more commonly by phone. The ATTORNEY should ask the EXPERT if he or she is very knowledgeable in the area of toxicology under litigation and whether he or she will be available. If at all possible, the EXPERT should be geographically close to where the trial will take place. The EXPERT should inquire about the ATTORNEY's timetable. (It is not wise to accept an assignment if the trial date is set within a few days, because there will not be enough time for the EXPERT to evaluate the case and do the necessary literature review.) The EXPERT should warn the ATTORNEY as soon as possible during the phone conversation that no confidential information should be revealed. The ATTORNEY will most likely ask the EXPERT about his or her fee schedule.

After the initial contact is made, and as soon as possible, the potential EXPERT should write a letter to the ATTORNEY. (Of course, the EXPERT must get the exact name and address of the ATTORNEY during that phone call; if the contact is by letter or fax, the address will be available from the letterhead.) The following is an example of the type of letter that should be sent:

Dear Mr. Attorney:

Thank you for your phone call of January XX, 19XX, telling me about your interesting case. I believe that I can be helpful to you on this toxicological problem. However, before I am certain, I will need some more information from you about the case at hand. Please send me a short summary of the complaint and other materials that will help me decide for sure if I can be helpful. Please do not send me any privileged information that would bind me to your case. What is your timetable; has a trial date been set yet?

After I receive your short summary, and if I consider myself an expert for your case and find I can be available, I will need a letter from you engaging me as either a consultant or as an expert witness. Both the opposing counsel and the judge usually ask for the exact date that I have been engaged by an attorney. Because I will have to put in some time to check the literature and evaluate the scientific merits of your case, I am requesting an advance fee for the first day after you engage my services. If for some reason I do not become your consultant or expert witness, I will return the fee.

Enclosed also are a copy of my curriculum vitae [or resume], a detailed schedule of my fees, an idea of my availability, a statement that I have no case in conflict with yours, and [optional] a resume of some of the toxic tort cases in which I have been associated.

Sincerely yours,

A. Toxicologist, PhD [or any other degree and the diplomate initials if applicable]

If the EXPERT and the ATTORNEY agree to the association, they should expect to work closely together.

WHAT YOUR ATTORNEY SHOULD TELL YOU

The very first step is for the ATTORNEY to decide if an EXPERT is really needed for the case under consideration. If the decision is to obtain an EXPERT, contact must be made at once. As noted previously, following the EXPERT's letter, the ATTORNEY should reply in writing requesting that the toxicologist become a consultant or witness on his or her case. The letter should have a brief outline of the duties, the dates when court activity is expected, and the compensation agreed upon. The letter should also have a cautionary statement of confidentiality. Some attorneys include suggestions for dispute resolution. Unfortunately, too few ATTORNEYS go to the trouble of writing such letters. The toxicologist, however, should be sure that these points are conveyed either in writing or orally. After all, the ATTORNEY–EXPERT relationship is symbiotic.

Your ATTORNEY should brief you on the nature of the case; you thus get the background of the problem as the ATTORNEY perceives it. The ATTORNEY should fill you in on what is known about the case, and what steps he or she has already taken to pursue the case. If other experts have been consulted, this fact should be revealed. If the ATTORNEY knows which other experts may testify for the LAWYER, this information should also be given.

Your ATTORNEY should tell you what the general and specific objectives of the case are. You must understand that the ATTORNEY can only give a limited amount of information. There may be a number of facts, for various reasons, that are not told to you at all.

The ATTORNEY may not discuss the monetary aspects of the case. You do not need to know how much the ATTORNEY is suing for or how many dollars the ATTORNEY is prepared to give the suing party to settle the case. Some ATTORNEYS give the EXPERT these figures; others do not. Because the EXPERT has no (or definitely should have no) financial stake in the outcome of a case, the dollar values should not be of concern.

What you as the EXPERT know about a case may be subject to discovery—and certainly will come out at the deposition and trial. A lack of certain details that are not instrumental in assisting you to form an opinion will not be a handicap for you and can protect the knowledge of the ATTORNEY.

If applicable, the ATTORNEY should clue you on what previous legal precedent has been set that pertains to the current trial. The ATTORNEY does not need (unless it will help you) to give references to specific court cases (e.g., *Jones v. Big Corporation*). The bare facts of the precedent should be enough to be useful.

The ATTORNEY should be specific about what is required in the way of communication from you as EXPERT to the ATTORNEY or from you as EXPERT to any other person the ATTORNEY designates. You should not take it upon yourself to communicate to another person using legal ideas or language, such as, "Be careful what you say to me, or what I tell you, because of the possibility of discovery." Such statements are not in the realm of the EXPERT. The ATTORNEY must be specific as to how reports are to be made—in writing, by fax, by telephone, or face to face. The ATTORNEY should remind you about confidentiality and that you must take every precaution not to give any confidential material to the opposing group.

If your ATTORNEY fails to give you the information that you believe necessary, you should not hesitate to ask outright. It is also important for you to accept the fact that there is not necessarily a lack of trust if the ATTORNEY does not satisfy your need for more knowledge or facts.

At one of the meetings the ATTORNEY should brief you, without insulting your intelligence, on some of the procedures that will be encountered in the courtroom. For example, the lawyer should mention such things as attitude, dress, mannerisms, and the like. Occasionally the ATTORNEY who engages an EXPERT forgets that the EXPERT is not an expert in the law that pertains to this case; it is incumbent on the ATTORNEY to explain the points of law that are applicable before the trial.

Although one of the main reasons for an ATTORNEY to engage an EXPERT is to have the EXPERT come to a conclusion and write an opinion from the facts of the case, sometimes an ATTORNEY asks the EXPERT to review the facts before a jury. A fact witness can certainly give the identical details, but many ATTORNEYS think the jury will be much more impressed if the EXPERT states them.

IS THERE PRIVILEGE?

Only under unusual circumstances can there be an ATTORNEY–EXPERT privilege. Both the ATTORNEY and the EXPERT should conduct themselves as though there is no privilege, because there may be no such protection. The LAWYER, by virtue of discovery, can learn all information the EXPERT provides to the ATTORNEY. However, specific situations can occur where privilege can be claimed. If the EXPERT is also a medical doctor and does actually examine the patient claiming injury, the medical records can be considered confidential, but court orders requiring disclosure can occur. In some cases, the EXPERT may look over very confidential documents that are labeled classified by the U.S. government; the ideas therein may be too technical to be expressed in lay language. In such cases, the information is considered privileged. The EXPERT may work for an ATTORNEY's client who claims that some information is proprietary and thus privileged. This excuse does not, however, cover information available in the course of normal business. In some cases, trade secrets can be placed in a sealed envelope, only to be opened as directed by the court.

Hint: If an EXPERT does claim the information at hand is privileged, the ATTORNEY may be wise not to call the EXPERT to testify but to make him or her a nontestifying expert. Privilege does apply to consultants, nontestifying experts, and potential witnesses who are not named as EXPERT witnesses.

On the other side of the coin is another question: Can the ATTORNEY sue the EXPERT for professional negligence because he or she did not provide adequate support services? So-called "litigation privilege" protection depends on the state; it is not uniform throughout the United States. Historically, British common law set the precedent for immunity of the testifying EXPERT in judicial proceedings. Originally, the protection was to prevent an EXPERT from being sued for statements made during interrogation in a trial. Some states extend the privilege covering claims against the EXPERT to include claims of misrepresentation, negligence, and, in extreme cases, perjured testimony. Court-appointed EXPERTS are especially protected.

It is rare (but not unknown) for an ATTORNEY to sue a friendly EXPERT. This happens especially if the ATTORNEY believes the EXPERT has failed to give adequate information during the pretrial preparation; negligence may therefore be claimed. There can be no protection for mistakes! Some judges have stated that if EXPERTS are subject to possible damage suits, their testimony may be distorted to favor one party or another, and thus the fact finder is deprived of reliable and objective evidence. Along the same line, some courts have ruled that, as a matter of law, an EXPERT serves the court and it is the court that decides the boundaries in which an EXPERT can testify. The fact that the EXPERT is retained and paid by an ATTORNEY does not alter the fact that the EXPERT is an active participant in the judicial proceeding.

The future of privilege is not clear; claims of malpractice against ATTORNEYS' own EXPERTS are still being fought in different states. One good hint for an EXPERT is to be careful of accepting a case when he or she has testified in a similar situation, but on the other side.

WHAT IS DISCOVERY AND DISCOVERABLE?

Discovery is a pretrial set of procedures, and there are rules relating to discovery (e.g., *Rules of Civil Procedure*, Rule 26; General Provisions Governing Disclosure; Duty of Disclosure). The ATTORNEY should advise the EXPERT what is required, including limitations and exceptions. Discovery is one of the first phases of the pretrial; it is the means used by either party in a case to obtain facts and information about the case from the other party. This information is needed for the preparation for the trial. The sharing and exchanging of information may not be as complete as either side wishes. (Learn as much as you can; tell as little as you must.) The client must be represented in the best possible manner. Civil rules of discovery are more general than those for criminal cases. In the latter, there is a constitutional protection against self-incrimination.

The philosophy behind the discovery process is to permit the two parties to arrive at the truth, to prevent perjury, and to detect fraudulent as well as sham claims (and defenses). This process educates both sides prior to the trial as to the true value of the claim. Discovery can facilitate settlement, speed up litigation, avoid surprises, and limit the issues. Discovery is not simple. Many lawyers go beyond obtaining documents by delving into the private lives of the opponents.

There are limits imposed on the discovery process. All lawyers' (not EXPERTS') work is free from discovery; an ATTORNEY's notes, analysis, and trial strategy are privileged. The ATTORNEY's letter to the EXPERT is also work product, if so labeled. Any communication between an ATTORNEY and a consultant who is not to be a trial witness is also privileged. If, however, the consultant later becomes a testifying EXPERT, there will be problems related to discovery; this is the reason it is essential to note the exact date that a consultant is designated an EXPERT. Before this date, the EXPERT can purge his or her files, consolidate notes, and toss out irrelevant materials. This is not considered unethical.

What is included in discovery? All written reports of an EXPERT (but not of a consultant or nontestifying expert) fall into this category. All documents (which may not be complete or comprehensive), depositions, interrogatories, and testimony, if available, are subject to discovery. Even results of physicians' examinations, both physical and mental, can be revealed in discovery, if so ordered by the court; this despite the claim of physician–patient confidentiality. Ideally, expert witnesses never write down any notes, or ideas or opinions, and contact the ATTORNEY only by phone. Materials should be written only at the specific request of the ATTORNEY.

The implication for the EXPERT is that anything written, be it personal notes, short communications to the ATTORNEY, or formal reports, must all be shared. The ATTORNEY must give guidance to the EXPERT on how to deal with audio- and videotapes.

In this computer age, much information is kept on computer disk. As information becomes more complete, documents are altered and edited on the screen; previous versions become unavailable. It is unclear at this time whether computer files must be shared. If software is developed for special documents, is the disk to be part of discovery? When will the Internet, e-mail, and the World Wide Web be involved? These subjects must be discussed with the ATTORNEY.

If the LAWYER asks for the EXPERT's entire file, you should immediately consult with the ATTORNEY prior to complying to this request.

Naturally, the ATTORNEY will want to review your files and help you identify all materials that are responsive to any request for information from a LAWYER. However, as an EXPERT, you can be in trouble if you are not in complete control of the documents. Be careful to note what, if any, material the ATTORNEY removes from the files. Should any relevant material be removed by the ATTORNEY, a question of ethics can arise. You must request that the ATTORNEY provide a written list of the material removed from the files.

What should be the disposition of completely new information if found after the discovery exchange takes place?

WHAT EXPERIMENTS?

At times, the EXPERT must consider whether actual experiments should be conducted in a laboratory. This decision must be made early in the pretrial process. Questions then arise as to whether the experiment should be conducted by the EXPERT or contracted to a commercial laboratory. The ATTORNEY must be informed of the EXPERT's recommendation.

Experiments Done by Others

It is the obligation of the EXPERT to make a thorough literature search to determine whether the proposed experiment has already been carried out by some other laboratory. Some data are already available; for example, an acute median lethal dose value (LD_{50}) must have been determined for almost every chemical in commercial use. Data may also be readily found on dermal absorption, and even on toxicokinetics. A critical evaluation of the validity of the published work is in order.

If you as EXPERT determine that a special toxicological experiment is indicated, you should suggest where the laboratory work should be done. You should undertake to be the monitor of the work; if not, you should recommend an on-site monitor.

What To Do

No matter who does the experiment, complete records must be kept. Unimportant details may become important points in an open court. Every observation, every calculation, every measurement must be recorded. A bound (not looseleaf) notebook is essential, and every page must be initialed and dated. Every purchase must be noted, including: from whom, when, cost, purity (if a chemical), and amount obtained. Each item that you do not handle personally must be noted and recorded: Who actually touched the material? A note must be made to assure the court that no person substituted any agent during or after the experiment was completed.

HELP WITH INTERROGATORIES

Interrogatories are sets of written questions one party sends to the other, or to an individual such as the EXPERT who will give testimony at the trial. (There have been occasions when interrogatories have been sent to the wrong person.)

There appears to be no limit on the number or the nature of the questions asked. Often interrogatories are sent prior to a deposition; the answers can lead to further and more in-depth questions at the deposition. Answers must be provided within thirty days and under oath. The time frame can be flexible if both sides agree; otherwise, the court can make time adjustments. If by courtesy the LAWYER (or the court) does give an extension, it should be acknowledged in writing. If objections (quite often to state that some questions are not specifically related to the case now in court) are made to any of the questions, the ATTORNEY has forty-five days to complete the answers to the interrogatories.

Only when the ATTORNEY requests it, the EXPERT can be a great help in responding to technical questions. Usually the unimportant questions are answered more fully than the important ones! An EXPERT may also help the ATTORNEY construct the questions to be sent to the LAWYER. The purpose of interrogatories is to help each side learn who the opposing expert will be, the opinions of the opposing expert, and, in the main, what the opposing expert will testify to. The ATTORNEY should find out all about the opposing expert, and what his or her qualifications are. The EXPERT can be of help here, too: Is the opposing expert a member of a learned society; has the opposing expert published papers in this general or specific field? Such facts are more readily obtained by the EXPERT than the ATTORNEY.

Interrogatories may be used to answer the following questions: What did that EXPERT see, where, and when? What did the EXPERT do about the situation? What were the dates, times, and places? What conclusions were arrived at, and how? What opinions were formulated, and why? At times it is permissible to respond to a specific question with, "This question is too ambiguous," or "This question cannot be answered," or "This question can only be given a partial answer."

The EXPERT should remind the ATTORNEY, if the ATTORNEY has not already thought of it, which documents in the files may be relevant to answering the interrogatories.

Although the interrogatory process is, in effect, a fishing expedition, too many questions can give a clue to the opposite party about what avenue will be followed at the deposition. Caution must be taken to avoid the appearance that the deponent is too prepared.

Questions given to members or potential members of a jury are also called interrogatories.

ROLE OF THE PARALEGAL

The paralegal and the legal analyst have roles to play in the vast area of toxic torts. For one, the paralegal may help the ATTORNEY find the right EXPERT. After the EXPERT for a case has been designated, the paralegal can do a background check on the EXPERT. Photocopies of the EXPERT's publications can be obtained. The paralegal can often check the EXPERT's biography in any *Who's Who.* It may fall on the paralegal's shoulders to screen out the wrong expert.

Time after time, the paralegal can "baby-sit" the EXPERT. While the ATTORNEY is totally engaged in the trial proceedings, the paralegal can keep in touch with the EXPERT, coordinate schedules, arrange the appearance of the EXPERT in court at the proper time, and remain with the EXPERT until he or she is called in. The paralegal can take charge of any exhibit or special display materials. Also, the paralegal should have all details of the travel schedule of the EXPERT and should be able to contact him or her at all times.

Both the paralegal and the legal analyst can find references for the EXPERT. They can go over medical and technical reports with, and for, the EXPERT. Questions the EXPERT may have on a case can be considered by either the paralegal or the legal analyst.

Finally, paralegals and legal analysts can play important parts in a mock trial if the ATTORNEY decides to conduct one.

Chapter 4

What Do You Offer the Attorney?

Generally, an ATTORNEY hears about or knows a toxicologist and then makes contact with that individual as a potential testifying EXPERT. If the toxicologist does not know the ATTORNEY, it may be wise to check up on him or her through acquaintances or the comprehensive directory of lawyers; there is a listing for each state in the United States (*Martindale-Hubbell Law Directory* [121 Chanlon Road, New Providence, NJ 07972]), available in any law library. After the initial contact is made, a formal letter should be received by the toxicologist requesting that he or she be a consultant or an EXPERT. Even experienced experts fall into the trap of talking to an attorney, doing some preliminary work, and then getting a letter some time later such as the one below. (And then where is the fee for the time spent?)

Dear Dr. Expert:

It was nice talking to you the other day. The case is now settled and we will not need your expert advice now. Perhaps some later date we can use your expertise.

Sincerely Yours,

A. Attorney

If a potential EXPERT wishes to bill an ATTORNEY, no work should be done until the following are clarified:

- the fee schedule and its ramifications;
- whether the expert is hired as a consultant or an EXPERT;
- the exact date the ATTORNEY expects the EXPERT to start (which also may be requested by the judge or the LAWYER); and
- the scope of work to be done.

It is highly inadvisable to accept a rush assignment. Some ATTORNEYS call an EXPERT on Tuesday to come and testify on Thursday or Friday. Unless the EXPERT is up-to-date to the day, it is not wise to accept such a hasty commission.

The EXPERT often can offer the ATTORNEY information about the various other experts whom the LAWYER may use. Many toxicologists know each other and are often somewhat knowledgeable about each other's qualifications, good points, and "flaws." Sometimes the EXPERT may even know the opinions of the opposing EXPERT and suggest deposition questions for the ATTORNEY to ask.

Sometimes the EXPERT needs to obtain help from another scientist. The toxicologist may need more information on the method of analysis of an agent or on a complex mixture; a chemist is then consulted. He or she may need more information on the side effects of long-term medication with painkilling drugs; a pharmacologist or pharmacist is then consulted. The ATTORNEY must give guidance to the EXPERT on how this "outside" consultation should be described. In some states, the list of the EXPERT's consultants need not be revealed in the written opinion; many courts assume that scientists talk to one another.

What should the EXPERT do if the LAWYER asks, "Did you consult with another scientist when forming your opinion?" The EXPERT and ATTORNEY must anticipate this question; naturally, if another scientist was consulted, it should be admitted. Is a logical explanation needed?

What the EXPERT offers the attorney, in summary, is to educate the ATTORNEY on the science of the case and to fill in the gaps as necessary. The EXPERT can help draft questions for the interrogatories to be presented to the opposing LAWYER as well as help the ATTORNEY answer questions given to him or her. An EXPERT may suggest sources of information and evidence. Sometimes a consultant can help prepare another EXPERT whom the ATTOR-NEY wishes to retain. Finally, one of the most important functions an EXPERT performs is to give the ATTORNEY a scientific opinion based on the facts of the case.

EVALUATE THE STRENGTHS
AND WEAKNESSES OF THE CASE

The EXPERT should investigate every aspect of the case; he or she must read all written material (that the ATTORNEY wishes to have revealed). The EX-

PERT must evaluate the weaknesses as well as the strengths of the scientific case being prepared by the ATTORNEY. It is incumbent on the EXPERT to inform the ATTORNEY what, if any, are the defects of the case under consideration; this should only be done orally unless otherwise requested. Usually the ATTORNEY knows the strengths of the case. The EXPERT must be on solid ground when this topic is discussed. If at all possible, the EXPERT should have specific scientific references to share with the ATTORNEY on both the strengths and the weaknesses of the case.

Too often, the ATTORNEY does not ask for an evaluation by the EXPERT; the EXPERT is then treading on thin ice when this topic is considered. It is wise to discuss whether the EXPERT will be asked to point out the strengths and/or weaknesses of a case before the formal appointment as an EXPERT is made. After all, the EXPERT's role is not to be the bearer of good or bad news, only to be an objective evaluator.

At all times the EXPERT must be aware that there is no attorney–client privilege in the relationship between EXPERT and ATTORNEY. All written material, be it formal or simply notes, and possibly much conversation can be subject to discovery. Again, it is necessary to advise the EXPERT not to write anything to the ATTORNEY without a specific request by the ATTORNEY to do so. This advice does not apply to the consultant or the nontestifying expert.

YOUR OPINION[1]

The EXPERT must review the facts of the case in great detail. A literature search is normally in order. There are many toxicology databases available. Many libraries now are on-line to the National Library of Medicine; some independent companies do literature searching for a fee. The search strategy must be carefully thought out to yield pertinent information. Are there reports in the literature on similar cases?

Many personal meetings between the EXPERT and the ATTORNEY are absolutely necessary. It is in these meetings that the EXPERT should give the ATTORNEY the benefit of the EXPERT's evaluation of the case. All this should be done verbally. The EXPERT would be wise, however, to keep a written log of time spent (and what was done) to formulate the opinion.

Only after a request should the EXPERT tell the ATTORNEY the opinion or conclusion he or she has derived from the information available. A subtle point here is that the EXPERT is engaged by the ATTORNEY not to give an opinion, but to derive an opinion. The EXPERT must be assured—and be careful—that the ATTORNEY is not trying to buy an opinion. The statement of the opinion should be clear and concise: "The damage done to an individual or an entity is (or is not) related to the exposure to a specific substance or agent."

Sometimes an EXPERT writes a preliminary draft of the opinion. If so, the

---

[1]Many details relating to the expert opinion are given in Chapter 1.

word "Draft" must appear on the top of every page to show that this is not the final opinion. As time goes on, new facts or new publications may become available; this new information may require a modification or elaboration of the original opinion. In this case, a new formal report should be written, and at the beginning of the report should be the date and an explanation as to why the first opinion has been modified. (This latter precaution is not necessary if the report is not submitted elsewhere, because it is expected that more than one draft of an opinion will be written.)

The ATTORNEY may have a specific format that the EXPERT should use. The ATTORNEY can help the EXPERT state his or her opinion in legal language, or any other terms, but only if the ATTORNEY thinks it is necessary. For example, phrases like "more likely than not," "with a great deal of scientific certainty," and "by a preponderance of evidence" are not common usage among toxicologists. Under no circumstances should the EXPERT permit the ATTORNEY to put words in the EXPERT's mouth, the nature of which may slant the opinion. A copy of the opinion may be sent to the LAWYER as a result of the discovery process; if the EXPERT is not expected to go to trial, his or her opinion can be limited and may not be revealed for discovery. The written report stating the opinion in clear words is one of the most important documents, because it can help the ATTORNEY decide to settle, drop, or take the case to court.

The final report must look professional. Handwritten reports should be avoided; a good word processor is in order. The report should have a cover sheet giving the following information: the EXPERT's name, address, phone number, fax number and e-mail address; the names and addresses of the client and the ATTORNEY; and the title and court number of the case. The first page of the narrative should review the problem and the claim of injury. These statements should be followed by the EXPERT's evaluation and a clear statement of the opinion and/or conclusion derived by the EXPERT. If necessary, pertinent references should be cited, and, if applicable, charts, diagrams, and photos (or photocopies) should be appended.

In court, if you are asked, "Do you have an opinion?" the answer should be one word: "yes" or "no." Do not elaborate at this time. When then asked, "What is your opinion?" make a simple statement, of perhaps one sentence, giving the court the benefit of the conclusion reached. Again, do not elaborate at this point. The ATTORNEY should then ask whether you believe the factual premises are true and if your opinion is based on them. After you reply in the affirmative, the ATTORNEY should ask the reason, or basis (or some such word), for the opinion. Only then should you go on as long as you wish to explain the details of the facts and ideas behind the opinion. Too many EXPERTS try to give too many details at first without being asked. The LAWYER loves this.

One of the ATTORNEY's objectives is to have the EXPERT demonstrate to the jury the reliability of the facts in the case. Scientific biomedical journal articles should be the backbone of the opinion; many judges do not allow lay magazine stories to be used to back an opinion. Specific references to recognized biomedical journals are the most acceptable.

Opinions of other experts can be used if they are explicitly recorded in a deposition or scientific publication; on the other hand, opinions based solely on the conclusions of other scientists are not acceptable. It is difficult to determine how circumstantial evidence can be used; the guidance of the ATTORNEY is important here. What the EXPERT must resist is the request of an ATTORNEY for the EXPERT to introduce inadmissible evidence under the pretense of explaining the reason for the opinion.

Above all, the opinion stated by the EXPERT must be based upon both known facts and scientific probability. In light of the Supreme Court's *Daubert* decision, the EXPERT must demonstrate the validity of the analysis and conclusions. Some states require that the written opinion be given to the jury.

In the last analysis, an opinion is not a fact. Once you have stated an opinion, stand by it. If badgered, hold your ground and say, "That, Sir [or Ma'am] is my expert opinion."

DO YOU HELP WITH THE LAW?

The function of the EXPERT is to provide the expertise on the science of the case; the function of the ATTORNEY is to provide the expertise on the law. The two are not, however, mutually exclusive. The ATTORNEY may wish to become knowledgeable about the science of the case. The various EXPERTS may be asked to present seminars for the ATTORNEY, and also for interested associates and paralegals on the case.

If the EXPERT knows some legal precedents, this information should be disclosed during one of the many discussions with the ATTORNEY. Such an EXPERT may even suggest some litigation strategy to the ATTORNEY.

Your ATTORNEY should explain any important laws and decisions that will pertain to the case. You and your ATTORNEY should review the function of an EXPERT witness in accordance with the FRE, the Frye Rule, and the recent decisions of the Supreme Court. A clear understanding of the rules will enable you to be a better witness. Also, it will help you to evaluate the credentials of the EXPERT witnesses on the opposing side.

CAN YOU DO EXPERIMENTS?[2]

The answer is yes—with some caveats. The toxicologist must demonstrate that he or she has a previous record of doing experiments in the special field of interest, or in a closely related field. A toxicologist who has published solely or mainly on toxicokinetics may not be acceptable to a judge if the experiment performed is quantification of tetrahydrocannabinol in a marijuana plant.

[2]This section complements the material in Chapter 3.

If experiments are to be conducted, then the guidelines for good laboratory practice must be followed. It is most important to pay attention to details. A good *bound* notebook must contain complete specifics of the procedure to be followed and exact notes if modifications are made. Every page must be dated, signed, and witnessed by another individual. No pages must be torn out. It is acceptable to write "void" over a page; but that page must not be destroyed. Nothing should be erased; a single line through a word or phrase is adequate. Sometimes it is wise to note in the margin of the page why it has been "voided."

Problems will arise if the experimenter fails to keep a record of the chain of custody. Notes and dates must be kept of all persons involved in every aspect of the experiment. When and where were supplies obtained or purchased? Who handled the material, for how long? Where were supplies kept? Details of the experiment are needed. Who else handled any supplies in your experiment? Where is the final product stored? What evidence does the toxicologist have that the experiment was completed in accordance with good science? It is important to let the jury know that in no way was the experiment "doctored" to get specific results.

As the EXPERT, you must be prepared to show the LAWYER all records. In the case of a product, you must be convincing that there was no chance for anyone to substitute anything along the way.

You must educate the ATTORNEY as to what was done and why. The ATTORNEY should also be briefed on areas of research that do not pertain to the experiment conducted. You and the ATTORNEY must spend time thinking about what questions the LAWYER can ask relative to the experiment.

There are times when your side may need to have experiments conducted; however, you may not be the one to conduct them. If you must testify about experiments conducted by others, it is best to be present and see the work being done first hand. The experimenter should note in the record book that you were present throughout the procedure.

LIMITATIONS

From the onset, it is essential that the court know precisely what is the area of EXPERT's expertise; the limitations of that expertise, however, can come out during testimony. It is also possible for the ATTORNEY to tell the court that the EXPERT is conversant with another subspecialty, such as teratology.

The toxicologist must be wary, and as an expert witness should not try to be all things to all people. It is very easy to succumb to the pressure from one's own ATTORNEY to testify as an EXPERT in a variety of toxicological fields. Too often, the ATTORNEY will try to flatter the EXPERT by saying, for example, "Of course you are more knowledgeable in areas A, B, and C than other toxicologists I could ever engage."

Many ATTORNEYS wish to save money and have one toxicologist testify on teratology, epidemiology, pathology, carcinogenesis, risk assessment, addiction, and more. This is not a good idea for the toxicologist. Juries frown on EXPERTS who cover too many diverse topics and appear to be global experts. A good rule of thumb is that a toxicologist should be qualified as an expert in the major field of toxicology, and at the most two subspecialties, such as carcinogenesis and teratogenesis. Risk assessment can fall within the major field. It is incumbent on the ATTORNEY, perhaps with the aid of the EXPERT, to find other specialists who can discuss areas such as public health, occupational exposures, special diseases, industrial hygiene, or even other subspecialties within toxicology.

If the ATTORNEY approaches an EXPERT to testify in a subspecialty of toxicology in which he or she is not comfortable and is not a real expert, it is best for the EXPERT to avoid being talked or flattered into accepting the assignment. For example, a toxicologist may have a good knowledge of the broad field of toxicology, but may not be a real expert in combustion toxicology, or pathological changes in an eye following exposure to an exotic chemical, or specifics of the role of a certain chemical in teratology.

In summary, within the limits of his or her expertise, a testifying toxicologist should be able to explain to a jury just what the discipline of toxicology encompasses. Its quantitative nature must be emphasized: Toxicology is a science that deals with the *amount* of an agent that causes an adverse action in some living system(s). The relation of toxicology to pharmacology should be carefully explained to the jury. The toxicologist, if qualified correctly, should be accepted as being well versed in the aspect of toxicology relevant to the particular trial, and, as stated, in perhaps two subspecialties. Primarily, the toxicology EXPERT should explain the general discipline. Many toxicologists are good mathematicians and can discuss the various mathematical models and extrapolations used for risk assessment. Some have expertise in modern subspecialties such as mechanisms of action, immunology, hemoglobin or nucleic acid–chemical interaction to form adducts, chromosome aberrations, peroxisome proliferations, and other newer disciplines.

This breadth of knowledge can impress colleagues, but not necessarily juries. In addition to the difficulty of qualifying a toxicologist in a number of subspecialties, an attempt to do so may have an adverse effect on the credibility of the toxicologist as an EXPERT witness. If the toxicologist does succumb and testify in too many fields, the LAWYER will attempt to cast doubt on his or her expertise in cross-examination. It will be easy for the LAWYER to characterize the EXPERT as a "jack of all trades but a master of none." The ATTORNEY, as mentioned, should engage other EXPERT witnesses for the presentation of the different fields to be discussed during the trial. If the ATTORNEY wants to save money by asking the toxicologist EXPERT witness to be all things to all people, it will prove to be a false economy.

A toxicologist, unless also a physician, cannot examine a patient who claims damages. The toxicologist cannot prescribe drugs. These facts should be clearly stated to the jury during qualification time. The toxicologist can look over medical records to aid the ATTORNEY in deciding how to proceed in a trial (or even whether the ATTORNEY has a real case). The toxicologist may know in general terms the toxic action of an agent, but may not know the specific details of the pathological effects on an exposed human. The EXPERT and ATTORNEY will have to decide to what extent the EXPERT should become a real expert on such subjects, or to refrain from discussing the subjects in any but general terms.

For example, the toxicologist may know in general the symptoms of chronic selenium poisoning, but may not know specific details such as the peeling of skin on the fingertips or toes, or the rotten odor of the exhaled methylated selenium.

The EXPERT may need help, but should avoid hiring a subcontractor unless there are unusual circumstances. If at all possible, the EXPERT should not get involved in or be responsible for the work or fees of other EXPERTS.

Some ATTORNEYS have asked toxicologists for advice in fields totally alien to their expertise, such as the psychological profile of an alleged victim of exposure, or even help with jury selection. Such requests should be resisted. Recall that some ATTORNEYS have sued their own EXPERTS for wrong advice. Because it is virtually impossible for a toxicologist to get malpractice insurance, the toxicologist must be careful at all times in giving advice out of his or her field of expertise.

CONFIDENTIALITY

An ethical toxicologist does not discuss the case in which he or she is involved with anyone other than the ATTORNEY or someone the ATTORNEY authorizes. No document should be shown to anyone outside of the intimate circle designated by the ATTORNEY.

At times, cases are interesting and even bizarre. The temptation to make remarks about a case to friends should be controlled. A slogan popular during World War II should be heeded: "Who is listening?"

DISPUTE RESOLUTION

No EXPERT likes to get into a dispute with the ATTORNEY who has engaged him or her. Realistically, sometimes disagreements do arise that require some drastic action on the EXPERT's part. Practically all such disagreements can be avoided if there is an exchange of letters. Either party can be the first to write. The EXPERT writing to the ATTORNEY about what the EXPERT can offer should include the EXPERT's fee schedule. The ATTORNEY writing a letter engaging the EXPERT should set the conditions of the relationship. If the ATTORNEY responds to the EXPERT's letter, this response should acknowledge the fee requested. Unfortunately, it has been estimated that fewer than half of parties take the trouble to write formal letters.

The types of difficulties most frequently encountered between an EXPERT and ATTORNEY are: unusual delays; unclear assignments; additional work beyond what was agreed upon; lack of information as to who pays the fee, and when; the ATTORNEY not paying the fee if a case is lost; and the ATTORNEY deciding unilaterally after a case is over to lower the fee.

The EXPERT can try to resolve a dispute over fees by writing to the local bar association and complaining, or by checking to see if there is an arbitration board in the local legal association. Perhaps negotiating a settlement is the least troublesome. Naturally, the EXPERT will sever relations with that ATTORNEY. In the last analysis, the EXPERT can simply accept the loss, or, as a last resort, the EXPERT can sue the ATTORNEY.

Chapter 5

Reports: To Be or Not to Be?

Reports, whether oral or written, can range from minimal to extensive. Many ATTORNEYS request reports other than opinion reports. This aspect depends on the needs of the ATTORNEY and must be discussed very early in the arrangement. By no means should the EXPERT ever send anything in writing until a request is made by the ATTORNEY!

ORAL VERSUS WRITTEN

It is best, at first, that communication between the EXPERT and ATTORNEY occur only in person or by telephone. Written material (including any fax) sent to the ATTORNEY is not confidential. As explained earlier, all documents and exhibits or material pertinent to the case can be examined by the LAWYER at discovery. Some courts have ruled that even the EXPERT's notes on the case may given to the LAWYER during the discovery process. The EXPERT must always keep in mind that all of his or her reports and written communications may be shown to the LAWYER.

If a report is requested, the EXPERT should be sure to get guidelines from the ATTORNEY. The report should list the facts as the EXPERT knows them, and any information obtained from other sources should be referenced. If the report is related to the opinion, above all, the opinion expressed must be clearly stated to be the EXPERT's own. The ATTORNEY may try to influence the EXPERT in some phase of the EXPERT's report to enhance the ATTORNEY's position and court strategy. This must be resisted.

WHAT DETAILS ARE IMPORTANT?

One suggested outline for a report is presented below. Everything must be dated; the order is not critical.

Title.
A brief statement of the problem attacked in this report.
A brief summary of the findings.
A short detailed report of the research done in the technical library.
Summary of laboratory work done (or supervised).
Some pertinent references.
Short sketches of any charts, diagrams, and the like that may be useful during the trial. These can be made up by a special chart or diagram maker.
A complete statement of the opinions derived.
All bases and reasoning used to come to the opinion.
All publications of which the EXPERT is an author. (Some may not be relevant to this case, but all should be included.)
The fee charged for this report.
A list of other cases for which the EXPERT gave a deposition or gave testimony at a trial during the previous four or five years.
A statement and signature attesting that this report was prepared by the EXPERT alone.

The EXPERT will in all probability be questioned by the LAWYER as to whether the report has been in any way influenced by the ATTORNEY or someone else who wants a favorable outcome for the case. The EXPERT should always remember that it is not his or her case; the EXPERT is not the ATTORNEY.

In addition to reports, the handling of personal notes must be discussed early in the process. All EXPERTS should review their habits with regard to notes: Do they keep and file notes? Do they take notes to refresh their memories of conversations and of material read in books? Do they take notes, review them, and then throw them out? All of these questions must be discussed early on. EXPERTS need guidelines for every case, because different ATTORNEYS have different ideas about how to deal with these topics. Each time the EXPERT writes anything, that section should be dated.

The EXPERT must think ahead, because any notes made (for any reason) will invariably be given to the LAWYER during discovery or if subpoenaed.

Any notes made should therefore also be signed at the bottom of each page and dated. After the report is written, the notes can be destroyed.

The EXPERT must be prepared for the LAWYER to ask him or her to furnish all material on which the EXPERT has relied to come to a conclusion. This material may include photocopies of references, and even copies of the pages of books used. Photocopies of the title pages and the pertinent sections are sufficient. The EXPERT should not submit entire books, because they may not be returned. If the actual books are provided, the EXPERT should make it clear to both the ATTORNEY and the LAWYER that they must be returned to the EXPERT after the trial, but this does not always happen. It is wise to make notes and records of everything provided to the LAWYER. Some trials take over a year to get on the judge's calendar; it is easy to forget over that time exactly which books and returnable materials were given to the LAWYER.

VISUAL AIDS: PROS AND CONS

Visual aids are very dramatic if done right. They must be accurate. There are a number of companies that cater to the legal profession to produce charts, diagrams, and the like. Sometimes the LAWYER may ask the EXPERT who made the visual aids used in a trial.

A good visual aid can be very effective in getting the EXPERT's points and ideas across to the jury. At all times, any visual aid should be covered until used, and then left uncovered. Charts, graphs, diagrams, maps, and photographs are often used. If appropriate, models can be made and exhibited. Some EXPERTS use videotapes. These can be rather boring if not made well; if done professionally, they can be a powerful teaching tool. One advantage to videotapes is that they can be replayed. Virtual reality will, no doubt, one day become a tool for the EXPERT to use in the courtroom. However, an EXPERT should not make the material appear to be too expensive! Some members of the jury will wonder why the EXPERT "gilded the lily." Can the EXPERT be trying to take the jury's mind away from the substance and only see the picture? In one case, vivid computer animation was used so that the jury could follow a path of a runaway accident. The jury was not impressed and did not rely on the tape one bit.

If the EXPERT makes some of the visual aids him- or herself, they will carry much more impact with the jury, than, for example, photographs made by a professional photographer. However, any photographs used must be of very high quality and enlarged enough to be seen in the courtroom. Visual aids must be very simple, clear, and not crowded. One or two ideas, or at the most three, should be presented per chart. When using charts or diagrams, the EXPERT must be careful to stand on the side and not block the view of the jury. If the diagrams or charts are to be marked, the EXPERT should use colored markers and make all notations BIG! Charts can be used again for closing arguments.

The overhead projector is also useful. Transparencies are very effective, because the basic information can be on one sheet, and other sheets can be overlays to build up the story to be presented to the jury. The penultimate overlay sheet should not have the conclusion; the climax of the EXPERT's presentation should be giving the conclusion orally—and only then placing the final sheet on top. Needless to say, the overlays should not obscure the information given on the sheets below.

All visual aids must be created so as to aid the jury in understanding the science of the case. The decisions on how to make and present the visual aids should take into account the fact that these exhibits will go to the jury deliberation room without the EXPERT.

All this advice on visual aids is predicated on the assumption that the ATTORNEY has introduced the material into evidence and the court has assigned a number to it. If this is not the case, the judge may not permit the EXPERT to use the material. When referring to any visual aid, the EXPERT should use the number assigned to it when it was placed in evidence.

If at all possible, the EXPERT should avoid doing a laboratory experiment in the courtroom, and should *never ever bring a rodent into the courtroom!* If necessary, an experiment can be done in a clean, orderly laboratory and video-taped; this precaution will prevent an experiment from failing at the wrong time in front of a jury.

Chapter 6

How Much Are They Paying You for Your Testimony?

The potential EXPERT must be up front with the ATTORNEY concerning the fee schedule. The terms, caveats, and nuances must be spelled out in writing. Any tasks not to be included must be clearly stated in the beginning. Verbal communication always seems to be misunderstood. If a lawyer phones and asks the toxicologist for the fee schedule, the toxicologist may or may not wish to give this information over the telephone. If the toxicologist does do so, immediate verification by letter is prudent.

ON WHAT IS YOUR FEE BASED?

The toxicologist may quote a fee for an entire case (and even a group of cases). Most toxicologists, however, quote hourly rates. It is important to be clear about which rate is for what. Working at home may be at one rate; meetings and research time in a different city may command another. Rates for depositions and court appearances may be two or three or times more than the working-at-home rate. Some cases go to arbitration; some experts have an arbitration rate different from the deposition or court appearance rate. The National Forensic Center has published examples of fees quoted for various services by various EXPERTS.

The EXPERT must be precise on what reimbursement is expected for travel expenses. If a toxicologist must fly to a different city, should coach, business, or first class travel be used? What types of hotels are acceptable? Should the day of travel be charged? Some toxicologists bill for it; some do not.

Details of billing are also important. Should the EXPERT bill monthly or at the end of the project? Normally, bills are itemized. Some ATTORNEYS want just a single sum on the bill with no details. The ATTORNEY's advice is necessary here, because this information will be part of discovery. One can expect that all written communication will get into the hands of the LAWYER.

Should the EXPERT demand a partial fee before starting any work on the case? There have been times when an ATTORNEY signed up an EXPERT but did not use him or her. One objective for "tying up" the EXPERT is to keep the opposing side from using that person. An "up front" partial fee indicates the true intention of the ATTORNEY.

BASIS FOR CHANGING THE FEE

The time period of the fee schedule should also be stipulated. Is the rate for one or more years? If it is not stated, there can be a misunderstanding. Sometimes a toxicologist is first asked to be a consultant or simply to do a literature search, but later becomes the EXPERT to appear in court; fee changes may be made. If an ATTORNEY loses a case and asks the EXPERT to lower the fee, it will appear as though the EXPERT has arranged a contingency fee, which, as noted, is unethical.

If a new ATTORNEY (or new firm) takes over a case, the EXPERT must, at once, discuss the agreed-upon fee; it may remain the same (and this should be understood) or modified.

IMPORTANT HINTS ON FEES

The most frustrating aspect of the EXPERT–ATTORNEY relationship is the time it takes for the ATTORNEY to pay the bill. When the EXPERT discusses the fee schedule with the ATTORNEY, the EXPERT should be told when and by whom the fee will be paid. Some attorneys pay monthly, others quarterly, and some prefer to wait until a trial is over and their settlement is completed. This process may take months or years, in which case the EXPERT may add an interest clause. Many ATTORNEYS have multiple insurance companies as clients, and the fee may be prorated among these companies. The ATTORNEY may make the EXPERT wait to obtain the fee until each company has paid its share of the expenses. In some liability suits, there may be an appeal; compensation may not be made for years. When submitting a bill, it is best to specify when payment is expected. It is incumbent on the EXPERT to be explicit on how he or she will bill the ATTORNEY and to render a detailed bill.

If additional work is necessary, it is essential to keep the ATTORNEY or insurance company apprised of this fact, and, if possible, to give an estimate of time and costs.

The jury is usually not surprised nor bothered by the size of the EXPERT's fee. Most of the members of the jury realize an EXPERT does not work an eight-hour day and that consulting is part-time.

The EXPERT may decide to wait until the entire case or project is completed before submitting a bill. This tactic can sometimes impress a jury and be a favorable factor in the courtroom, but not always.

Occasionally an EXPERT is so emotionally involved with the issue under litigation that this EXPERT may tell the LAWYER, and hence the jury, "I so believe in this issue that I am testifying without requesting a fee." The jury is totally unimpressed with this tactic!

Sometimes a LAWYER will try to make an issue of the fee the EXPERT charges for his or her time and expenses. If the LAWYER brings up the question of the fee, the following can take place: The LAWYER will ask (or shout), ". . . and how much are they paying you for this case?" It is correct to say, "I do not know." The immediate follow-up question will be, "Why don't you know?"

The EXPERT should then explain that the fee depends on the time spent on the case and "out-of-pocket" expenses. At this point, the EXPERT does not have all the information—how much time will be spent on the case in total. For example, the ATTORNEY may ask for more information after the EXPERT's testimony. Prior to a trial, this possible question should be discussed with the ATTORNEY and the answer rehearsed.

If you are asked by the LAWYER about your rate, give the fee schedule. Cross-examination on fees is not improper. Do not appear apologetic; just give the figure without elaboration or excuses. The members of the jury understand that an expert must be compensated. In practically all cases, every member of the jury has paid large doctor bills, and even plumbing bills, and thus expects an expert's fees to be high. The jurors do not compare their jury fee to yours. However, truly outlandish figures are met with raised eyebrows. Emphasize that a consultant may only work a limited number of hours or days. Most, but not all, jury members will understand.

Much more important than fees is the message to the jury, which you should convey in a calm manner: *Your opinion is your own.* It is based on the facts of this case, your evaluation of the scientific literature, and your experience and expertise. No one has influenced you in coming to a conclusion. You give an unbiased opinion, which may or may not help your ATTORNEY's client! You emphasize your charge for your time, but not your opinion. Do not let the LAWYER stop you; if necessary, appeal to the judge to let you finish. At all times, when you talk about this aspect, keep eye contact with different members of the jury.

The jury may wish to know who actually hired you to be a consultant or EXPERT. You must know who will pay your fee, the ATTORNEY or the ATTORNEY's client. Who will issue and sign the check?

At some time during your negotiation of your fee, there should be a written understanding regarding under what circumstances either party can terminate the agreement. Some ATTORNEYS have a boilerplate contract agreement to be signed. Read it carefully, and feel free to make any changes you wish. At times, it may be wise to have your personal attorney read and review the contract with you.

By no means can an EXPERT have a financial (or even a professional or ideological) entanglement in a case. It is absolutely unacceptable for an EXPERT to agree to a fee on contingency or based on a sliding scale, depending on the financial outcome of the case for the ATTORNEY. In some areas a contingency fee is illegal. If an EXPERT does accept a percentage of the settlement, that information will eventually come out in another case. That EXPERT will probably never be called upon again by an ethical attorney.

Some final notes on fees: The EXPERT is expected to render an *opinion* on a case. A chiropractor was hired as an EXPERT in a case. However, the chiropractor's testimony revolved only around the diagnostic problem of the patient; no real opinion was asked or given. The court ruled that this chiropractor was merely a fact witness and therefore not entitled to an EXPERT's fee.

One medical expert found that attorneys were listing his name on their panel of witnesses without his prior permission. He instituted a policy of charging $500 whenever he finds this unauthorized use of his name.

Chapter 7

Playacting

The ATTORNEY may wish to carry out a mock trial to acquaint the EXPERT with as much information about the case as the EXPERT needs to know. This "playacting" will also be of help to the ATTORNEY and the associates in planning the strategy to follow at the pending trial. Paralegals can be of great help here; among their other duties is to help educate the novice EXPERT on procedure.

ATTORNEY PREPARES THE WITNESS

The ATTORNEY must explain what the case is all about to the EXPERT. It must be made clear what the ATTORNEY's goal is, as well as all the pertinent facts of the case. It is useful for the EXPERT to know the ATTORNEY's philosophy and some of the strategy to be used in conducting the trial. It is not necessary for the ATTORNEY to give the EXPERT all of the details; for example, as noted before, the ATTORNEY may not believe it necessary to discuss the financial considerations of the case.

Early on, the ATTORNEY must let the EXPERT know if the court case is civil (party A suing party B, whether individuals or companies) or criminal (the government acting as the prosecutor against a person or a company). Rules of what can be entered as evidence differ for these two types of cases.

It is assumed that the ATTORNEY will have already questioned the EXPERT about the EXPERT's knowledge of court procedures. At this stage, the ATTORNEY should have a chance to question the EXPERT using questions that will be also asked in the courtroom.

The ATTORNEY should give the EXPERT a chance to rehearse the answers to these questions. The ATTORNEY should have a list of questions prepared, but should not necessarily give the written questions to the EXPERT. The ATTORNEY must listen to the EXPERT's responses and be satisfied that the EXPERT answers the questions in an understandable manner. The EXPERT must be careful, however, that the ATTORNEY does not coach him or her; what is said must be in the EXPERT's own words.

The ATTORNEY must tell the EXPERT how much or little legalese should be used, for example phrases like "more likely than not." The distinction between *possible* and *probable* must be clarified. The EXPERT should be advised about use of the term "with reasonable certainty."

Continuous Updates

The EXPERT and ATTORNEY should be in contact with each other periodically. If the EXPERT finds a new reference that may be useful to this particular case, the EXPERT should notify the ATTORNEY—verbally. The ATTORNEY should tell the EXPERT how this new information is to be received—by report, by note, by fax, by mail, or however.

In turn, the ATTORNEY should update the EXPERT on a variety of topics. These can include (among others) any new approach to the case, the ATTORNEY's need for new information or literature searches, and the ATTORNEY's new schedule relative to a new court calendar. Phone calls, even if infrequent, are in order.

If Indicated, a Mock Trial

Depending on the ATTORNEY's needs, available time, and evaluation of the pending trial's importance, a full-scale mock trial may be conducted. In this case, another attorney should act as a judge; law firm personnel (usually non-lawyers) can act as jurors. The ATTORNEY should act as the ATTORNEY in the case, and some colleague should act as the LAWYER. Formal trial procedures should be followed. The LAWYER should really try to harass the EXPERT, invalidate the EXPERT's answers, and in every way expose the EXPERT to tactics the real LAWYER may use.

This experience will give the EXPERT an opportunity to face the fire and learn what makes juries take notice. A hostile practice cross-examination will help the EXPERT to learn to listen carefully to questions, formulate his or her thoughts, and above all be more articulate in answering questions to the point.

At the end of the mock trial, there should be a good postmortem session.

The good and bad points should be discussed and analyzed. Each party will thus learn something for the future trial. These benefits can be enhanced if the mock trial is recorded on videotape.

THE HYPOTHETICAL QUESTION

During the trial, the ATTORNEY, or more often the LAWYER, will pose a hypothetical question to the EXPERT. Such questions start by giving certain interpretations of information and assume these hypotheses are facts. However, the assumed "facts" must (should) be within the scope of the case and must be limited to the facts in evidence. The EXPERT is not expected to add additional "facts." The EXPERT is asked to comment on the hypothetical situation and to draw a conclusion as to whether, for example, a person was exposed to a chemical and this exposure resulted in permanent injury to the lungs. Often the court itself can limit what is presented as a hypothetical question; this is to prevent the EXPERT from giving an opinion based on guesswork or conjecture.

The judge has authority to deal with the form, content, and use of the hypothetical question. Many judges use this prerogative, because a hypothetical question can be so worded as to be misleading, or much too speculative. The result can be to confuse a jury. The EXPERT should not be placed in a position to answer with a simple "yes" or "no" a hypothetical question with many clauses. The "facts" should be related to those that can be verified in acceptable scientific publications.

A poor question, for example, would be: "Let me pose a hypothetical question: Let us assume that this middle-aged woman was exposed yesterday to hydrochloric acid fumes; this is *extremely toxic*. In your opinion, will this exposure contribute to her inability to bear children?" Because this hypothetical question may contain a scientific absurdity (the woman may be past the child-bearing age), asking it of the witness should not be permitted. Another example of an absurd question would be: "Can you explain why people with silver–mercury amalgam dental fillings are more readily addicted to smoking than people without silver fillings?" This can be an example of junk science.

The framing of hypothetical questions can be very complicated and requires great skill. The EXPERT can be of service to the ATTORNEY in this regard by helping formulate such questions. The questions and thus the answers should be scientifically plausible but worded in language the jury can understand. The scientific theories must be presented, and the "facts" must be woven in. Hypothetical questions must be properly framed so that the questions and answers will assist the jury to have a better grasp of the truth. The LAWYER can frame hypothetical questions related to the presented evidence; a new or modified theory can be proposed within this framework. Evidence not related to the trial cannot be presented in hypothetical questions. A good question can improve the quality of the EXPERT's communicated information.

Hypothetical questions are posed to help one party and weaken the opposing side; these questions are to:

- sort out the facts of the case (even though they are presented as hypotheses) and analyze the evidence;
- give the court the benefit of the EXPERT's opinion as it pertains to the "facts";
- help the jury understand the "facts" of the case, by testing the accuracy and reasonableness of the EXPERT's testimony;
- help the jury understand what truth should be acceptable to them so that they can come to a logical and intelligent decision;
- strengthen the position of the EXPERT (if the hypothetical is presented by the ATTORNEY) or impeach the EXPERT (if it is presented by the LAWYER);
- contradict the testimony of an opposing EXPERT;
- demonstrate that the EXPERT's opinion is (or is not) consistent with the theory he or she has relied upon; and
- confuse the jury if the case is going badly for one party or the other.

Either the ATTORNEY or the LAWYER can attempt to use hypothetical questions to introduce unacceptable evidence, under the guise of clarification but in reality designed to present a conclusion that will help his or her side. Also, it should be noted that some hypothetical questions can be so ambiguous or vague as not to be answerable at all.

If one EXPERT's answer to a hypothetical question is contradicted by the opposing EXPERT, the court and the jury may have difficulty in understanding that there can be a valid scientific hypothesis, but that its interpretations, and hence opinions, can differ. During the mock trial, the ATTORNEY should ask such a hypothetical question and listen to the answer. The question should then be rephrased to give the EXPERT more practice in answering. This practice session will give the ATTORNEY another chance to hear and learn of the logic of his or her EXPERT, and how well (or poorly) the EXPERT speaks before an audience.

Chapter 8

Can You Determine Cause?

There is a major difference between the toxicologist's concept of scientific "proof of cause" and the legal profession's understanding of what constitutes "cause." Here the EXPERT and the ATTORNEY must be aware of each other's ideas on the subject of the definition versus the connotation of "cause."

DIFFERENCE BETWEEN SCIENTIFIC CAUSE
AND LEGAL CAUSE

To prove that an injury is the result of exposure to any agent is more difficult than relating an injury to, for example, an automobile accident. The toxicologist, or any other scientist, will find it necessary to consider a number of disciplines before concluding that the pathology demonstrated (or imagined) is the result of exposure to a specific agent or agents. For the attorney, it is sufficient to consider clear and convincing evidence and rely on probability—that is, it is more likely than not that the injury is the result of exposure to the agent. In other words, the function of science is to learn facts and apply the scientific method; the purpose of law is to resolve disputes and provide justice. Legal sufficiency overrides scientific certainty.

For the unsophisticated testifying toxicologist, the terms "possibility" and "probability" are not carefully separated. This is especially important when potential future injury from exposure to an agent is the main theme of a lawsuit. Many injuries are possible. Is there a remote possibility that an injury will occur in the future? Is there a reasonable certainty that the injury will occur? Courts will consider a case if an EXPERT quantifies the reasonable probability that harm will result from exposure. To some courts the idea of "beyond a reasonable doubt" means a 90% probability. In a civil suit, the court can accept the "preponderance of evidence," which means a jury must find the allegations more probable than not, and 51% probability is sufficient.

It is not in the toxicologist's realm even to consider the area of "contributory negligence." This aspect of the case should be consigned to the legal profession.

HOW DO YOU DETERMINE PROOF?

If a plaintiff claims harm from exposure to any agent, that plaintiff must demonstrate that the activity, or the product produced or sold by the defendant, is the direct cause of the personal injury or the property damage. The complication here is that there may be a long latency period before the injury manifests itself.

To approach the problem of proof may require the toxicologist to evaluate conclusions from epidemiological studies if they are available. Should there be animal experiments conducted on the agent in question, the toxicologist must first determine if these experiments are valid, and if so then consider these data in the determination.

Before commenting on the evidence, the toxicologist must be aware, as is the pharmacologist, that there may be a particular individual in a population who reacts uniquely to an agent. For example, although side effects can be predicted for most prescription drugs, once in a while a patient on medication may exhibit a totally unpredictable reaction, an *idiosyncratic* reaction. Such a reaction can occur after exposure to any agent, even water.

The scientist must be aware of junk science when attempting to determine cause. Too often there are witnesses on the fringe of medical specialties who appear to offer inappropriate diagnoses in support of injury claims. One can even expect some of these pseudoscientists to argue about chemically induced AIDS, the deliberate manipulation of a virus to produce the mutant AIDS virus. Even interpretations of electromagnetic fields' action on biological systems are subject to junk science, which the toxicologist may encounter in the courtroom.

MATHEMATICAL ASPECTS

Do You Act As an Epidemiologist?

Unless also an expert in this field, the testifying toxicologist should neither pose as an epidemiologist nor try to give a jury mathematical details of an epidemiological study. It would be unwise for the average toxicologist to get into an argument with a LAWYER about the meaning of the null hypothesis, or even the interpretation of the value $p < .05$.

On the other hand, after discussing this aspect with the ATTORNEY, it is logical for a toxicologist, even though not an expert in epidemiology, to raise questions about the conclusion of an epidemiological study. Was a hypothesis drawn before a study was made? Was the study conceived from sound biomedical knowledge, or did it come about because a computer found some type of correlation between exposure to an agent and a specific event (which might or might not have biological significance)? If so, what is the proof that a question was phrased before the mathematical work was done? These questions are important to strengthen (or weaken) the testimony of the epidemiologist.

Some epidemiologists have tried to equate association with absolute cause, and have tried to convince juries that their discipline can determine cause. The toxicologist should help the jury understand the difference between association and true cause—and that conclusions from an epidemiologic study cannot determine cause for a specific individual. The extrapolation of a numerical risk value of 3×10^{-6} to a specific individual is too problematic. A well designed epidemiological study at best can give an estimate of relative risk.

The toxicologist can educate the court about the meaning of the term "confounding factors," and ask how many pertinent confounding factors were considered, and how and why they were eliminated. Also, the toxicologist can help clarify the relationship of the results of animal experiments to the conclusions of an epidemiological study. Should the term "extrapolation" be used, or generalizations made, when relating experimental work to humans? Granted, experimental animals are not humans; but can conclusions from, for example, a teratogenic or carcinogenic study be related to human exposure?

The toxicologist can explain to a jury the major differences between a valid animal experiment and a study by an epidemiologist. Confounding factors of genetics, weight, disease, diet, and stress must all be controlled and noted by experimentalists, whereas epidemiologists realize that theirs is an observational science and must somehow compensate for confounding factors out of their control, such as other diseases. Their studies are not lifetime. Epidemiologists can eliminate a number of people from a study and thus skew the population and the results. In other words, the contrast is between observational versus experimental science. However, both disciplines have the same objective, to discover the effect of noxious agents on humans; in reality their approaches are not in conflict.

The EXPERT can also discuss a relatively new branch of science that helps permit the meeting of toxicology and epidemiology, namely molecular epidemiology. A qualitative explanation of the fusion of laboratory animal experiments and cancer epidemiology into molecular epidemiology may be in order. This explanation will require defining, in lay language, molecular dissymmetries such as adducts (detecting damage to DNA) as well as inherited cancer disposition, and how information from these two fields are related to cancer risk assessment.

Meaning of Risk Assessment

There is no doubt that the concept of risk assessment will be brought up in toxic tort cases. The jury must be educated on the difference between risk assessment and risk management; some will have heard of the latter in their place of employment. Perhaps it will be necessary to give working definitions of both risk and risk assessment. The former term can be defined as "the possibility of an injury, disease, or even death resulting from an exposure to an agent in the environment"; and the latter as "the estimate of the risk associated with a specific set of conditions: the existence of a hazard and the likelihood of being exposed to that hazard." Fundamentally, risk assessment is not only about mathematical formulas and graphs, but also about estimates, extrapolations, and assumptions. In its simplistic form, risk assessment is the attempt to estimate what level of exposure will do harm, or even be lethal, to humans from information generated by exposure of experimental animals to dose levels exceeding 100 to 100,000 times that measured in the environment.

The jury must be informed that there are at least four steps involved in conducting a risk assessment. First, there is the *hazard identification*, specifying that which can cause the harm. The U.S. Consumer Product Safety Commission, which was founded in 1973, provides the following working definition of a hazardous substance:

> [A] hazardous substance is any substance or mixture of substances which is toxic, corrosive or irritant, a strong sensitizer, flammable or combustible or generates pressure through decomposition, heat or other means, if such substance or mixture of substances may cause substantial personal injury or substantial illness during or as a proximate result of any customary or reasonable foreseeable handling or use, including reasonable foreseeable ingestion by children.

Next comes determination of the *dose–response* relationship. If the actual data are not available for this step, estimates are usually made. The U.S. Environmental Protection Agency has a database, known as IRIS, of the risk status of more than 500 chemicals; literature references are also available. Following the dose–response assessment is the third step, the *exposure assessment*. In this step it is necessary to describe the population exposed as well as the magnitude and duration of the exposure. The determination of the likelihood that humans will be so exposed is the *risk characterization*.

The dose–response relationship, with all of its ramifications, is one of the more difficult notions to explain to a jury of lay persons. The question can be asked, "Why cannot one look at a line and determine a dose–response relationship by measuring halfway down, or some such measurement?"

The problem is that the dose–response relationship is an S-shaped, or sigmoid curve. No matter how difficult, it is necessary for the EXPERT to explain that the origin of this curve is the different degree of response to a stimulus by a large number of people.

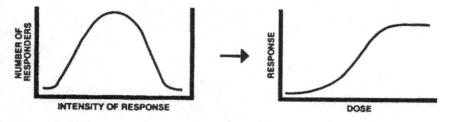

Figure 8.1   The bell curve and the sigmoid dose–response curve.

Some people are extremely sensitive to an agent, be it chemical or physical; a small number are very resistant to that same agent. The majority of the population are found in the middle of responders. If a graph is constructed with the number of responses against the intensity of response, a normal distribution curve will be generated. This is sometimes called a bell curve, or the Gaussian distribution curve (Figure 8.1, left). If intensity of response is instead plotted against varying dosages, the result is the sigmoid curve (Figure 8.1, right).

The extrapolation from a high dose to a low dose is very difficult; it can be approximated better if response is plotted against the log of the dose (Figure 8.2). The major problem is to estimate the dose–response relationship in the very low dose range, the shaded area in Figure 8.2. Government agencies have declared that there is no threshold dose for carcinogenic agents, whereas graphs have been constructed to estimate the threshold concentrations for noncarcingens. Different values are necessary for children and adults.

Various mathematicians have proposed relatively complicated formulas to deal with the gray area, the very low doses of carcinogenic agents. These alternate approaches have been graphed to give estimates of expected incidence of harm if exposed. For example, the expected number of cancers resulting from contact with a cancer-causing agent have been variously estimated through use

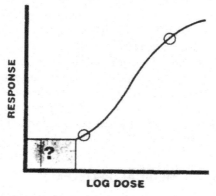

Figure 8.2 Dose–response curve based on log of dose. The major uncertainty is in the gray-shaded area.

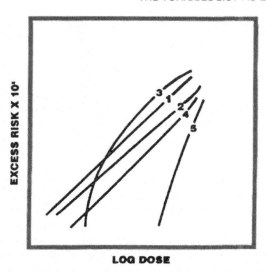

Figure 8.3 Various models attempting to relate excess cancer deaths to exposure levels. The models represented are: 1, one-stage; 2, multistage; 3, Mantel-Bryan; 4, Weibull; 5, log normal.

of different extrapolation curves. Models used in risk extrapolation have included: (a) distribution models: log-probit, Mantel-Bryan, logit, and Weibull; (b) mechanistic models: one-hit (linear), gamma multihit, multistage (Armitage-Doll), and linearized multistage; and (c) pharmacokinetic: time-to-tumor.

Figure 8.3 shows five of these models plotted on the same graph. In essence, they estimate excess risk of cancer versus exposure levels. It is of interest that, using the same database, they give estimates that differ from each other by factors of over 1000; which method used by the government depends upon how conservative the estimate is to be. The EXPERT can explain to a jury (as noted, in lay terms) that some agencies believe that an acceptable risk can be as great as 3×10^{-6}. The EXPERT will be wise not to give this numerical value to a jury, but to explain that such an agency will find a risk acceptable if only three persons in a million will develop cancer if exposed to a carcinogenic agent at a given level.

At present, U.S. government agencies are developing guidelines for risk assessment for noncarcinogenic endpoints such as mutagenicity, developmental toxicity, male and female reproductive toxicity, neurotoxicity, and immunotoxicity.

What may not be acceptable is for the EXPERT to initiate a discussion of comparative risks, relating the agent under consideration at the trial to exposure to completely different chemicals.

DO YOU TESTIFY ON MEDICAL PROBLEMS?

Very often the toxicologist is asked by the ATTORNEY to evaluate medical records. The EXPERT should suggest to the ATTORNEY what role he or she can play in litigation involving medical cases. So much depends on the "alter ego" of the toxicologist. If he or she has a good background in pharmacology, that discipline can be useful for discussing side effects and the potential long-term problems resulting from the continuous use of prescription medications. A background in chemistry can lead to testifying about the analysis of both legal and street drugs. It should be noted that there are precedents that permit a toxicologist who is not a medical doctor to discuss drugs, their actions, and their adverse effects.

With the introduction of the variety of complex and exotic chemicals into the environment, it can be expected that some sensitive individuals will have a severe reaction, either temporary or permanent, to a particular agent. Can the toxicologist explain to a jury the difference between an expected allergic reaction and one that is idiosyncratic? Some people are sensitive and react to nickel or chromium; can one associate an autoimmune disease with dermal exposure to either of these two metals? Can a toxicologist EXPERT present these concepts to a jury? Can the toxicologist testify about a "defective" product even if only a very few hypersensitive individuals have an adverse reaction when exposed? Also, if a person has an adverse reaction resulting from contact with an agent, should the toxicologist be able to testify on the absence (or presence) of adequate warning on a label?

In the last analysis, however, it is in the physician's purview, not the toxicologist's, to state that, to a degree of medical certainty, the plaintiff's injury was caused by the defendant's substance. The defendant's EXPERT can, however, testify that there is doubt that the specific injury claimed is the result of the specific level of exposure, or that the chemical form of the substance under question does not pose an unreasonable risk.

INTERACTION WITH ENVIRONMENTAL LAWS

Any chemical that is spread extensively throughout the environment, such as a pesticide, is subject to government licensing and regulations. Misuse of such an agent makes the user subject to penalties. The majority of claims of toxic harm to the environment are made by various government agencies claiming that the defendant has violated a regulation. Such suits are called "enforcement suits"; monetary penalties are often imposed, and cleanup may also be required. The money collected goes to the coffers of the agency. Occasionally, criminal liability is levied.

Toxicologists are often called in as EXPERTS by a defendant to explain why a particular agent is not to be classified as an environment hazard if used as directed. Government-employed toxicologists will argue the opposite.

Chapter 9

Now the Deposition

The deposition is oral testimony that the LAWYER takes prior to a trial. The deposition is one of the most important parts of a suit, because more than 90% of cases never go to court; suits are dropped or settled as a result of the quality of depositions. It will be helpful if the ATTORNEY gives the EXPERT a copy of a deposition taken previously of another EXPERT in a similar case (provided there are no restrictions against the EXPERT seeing this document). This will give the novice EXPERT an idea of what the final copy of a deposition looks like.

Long before the EXPERT's deposition is taken, much preparation should be made. The EXPERT and ATTORNEY must work together; the paralegal should also participate. The technical aspects and specific facts of the case must be reviewed, even if these subjects have been covered between these parties months before. If experiments have been conducted, the results and conclusions should be discussed as well. Pertinent references should be reviewed once again.

Also, before the deposition is taken, the EXPERT and ATTORNEY must confirm the dates of events. The LAWYER may rightfully ask questions such as, "On what date did the ATTORNEY ask you to become an EXPERT in this case?" "On what date did you form your opinion on this case?" "Were you a consultant before you were asked to be an EXPERT?" "Do you have similar cases with this or another firm?" "How many times have you testified for the defense in other cases?" and "How many times have you testified for a plaintiff?"

WHO CONDUCTS IT?

The LAWYER has the right to examine the EXPERT. The procedure is similar to a court appearance and has the same legal standing. The EXPERT must appreciate that at all times he or she is under oath. As a rule, in the absence of a jury as an audience, some of the usual pyrotechnics and posturing of the various attorneys will not take place. This does not mean that the LAWYER will not ask hostile questions or harass the EXPERT.

Your ATTORNEY and the LAWYER will set up a convenient time for your deposition. (Prior to this a subpoena may be served on you.) The place (never in your office!) is arranged by either the ATTORNEY or the LAWYER.

Your ATTORNEY and the LAWYER will be present, along with all other attorneys who have a stake in the outcome of the case, or who may otherwise have a professional interest. Also required to be present will be a court reporter, who should be a certified shorthand reporter as well as a notary public. This individual will administer the oath and then make a verbatim official record of all the questions and answers at the proceedings. If no court reporter can be present, the LAWYER and your ATTORNEY may elect to have an informal deposition taken; in this case, the LAWYER will question the EXPERT, but no official records will be taken, and the notes will not stand up in court.

There are times when, for some reason or other, it is not possible to assemble for a deposition. Under these conditions, a deposition may be taken and recorded on videotape. This tape can be played before the jury. Taping should be avoided, if possible, or used as the very last resort. Tapes are usually boring for a jury.

All EXPERT witnesses must be made aware that failure to appear for a scheduled deposition can be costly. It is possible for a judge to hold in contempt of court, levy a fine on, or even incarcerate the forgetful EXPERT. The judge has the prerogative of then barring the EXPERT from testifying at the actual trial.

WHAT IS IT, ANYWAY?

Perhaps the most important public appearance the toxicologist as an EXPERT witness will have is at the deposition. Why are depositions taken? Ideally, the main purpose is to see if enough evidence has been generated to settle a case without going to trial. In reality, the deposition is a fishing expedition. The LAWYER uses the deposition for at least four other reasons:

1   To learn what the EXPERT knows about the case or the facts of the case, with whom he or she has discussed this case, what tests he or she has made, and his or her opinion.

2   To learn much more about the science of the case. The EXPERT will supply valuable scientific information to the LAWYER.

3   To size the EXPERT up as a good or poor witness to oppose during a court trial.

4   To develop tactics later to discredit the EXPERT as a witness, or, if that is not possible, to make the EXPERT less effective before the court.

Because the EXPERT will supply valuable scientific information, the LAWYER must give him or her a fee. The fee for appearing at the deposition should have been previously arranged by the ATTORNEY; otherwise the LAWYER may write a check for the minimum amount set by the state. The LAWYER should hand over a check for the fee at least by the end of the deposition. If a check is not offered at that time, it is in order for the EXPERT to ask, in the presence of all the attorneys, when to expect his or her professional fee. Some EXPERTS will not even testify at a deposition (in spite of a subpoena) if a check is not forthcoming at once.

WHAT HAPPENS?

The procedure may vary from state to state, but the LAWYER starts the proceedings by introducing him- or herself. The LAWYER should ask you if you are familiar with depositions and the ground rules. (This question prevents an EXPERT from saying during the trial that he or she did not understand what was expected of him or her.) The LAWYER should be explicit in giving instructions about what is to take place.

Seated around the table, usually at some LAWYER's conference room or a rented conference room, will be the all the various attorneys whose clients have an interest in the case. Also present will be the certified court reporter. You as the EXPERT witness usually sit at the head of the table, and the court reporter sits next to you. Also sitting near you will be both the LAWYER and the ATTORNEY.

The LAWYER starts the proceedings. There are a few boilerplate questions asked at the beginning. The following narrative is typical of what takes place at a deposition (questions, Q, are by the LAWYER; answers, A, are by the EXPERT):

> **Q:** *Dr. Expert, I am John Lawyer. I represent Him, Her, & Me, an association of attorneys; we are the attorneys in this case. I have before me Exhibits marked "Witness-1" through "Witness-4." These pertain to your resume and letterhead, and some letters you sent or that were sent to you.*
>
> *Dr. Expert, I see you have a PhD after your name. I am in the habit of calling only those people doctors who have an MD after their name; however, if you are more comfortable being called doctor, or even professor, I will be happy to do so.*

A: *Either one, or Mr. Expert, will do.*

Q: *At various times I will call you doctor or professor.*

A: *Fine.*

[The ATTORNEY interrupts.]

ATTORNEY: *Do call him doctor, for that is the way we all know him.*

Q: *Now that we have gotten that formality over with, doctor, I am the attorney who represents the plaintiff (defendant) in this case. For the record, please state and spell your name.*

A: *Anthony Expert: E X P E R T.*

Q: *Have you ever participated in a deposition prior to today?*

A: *Aha, I have some time back. I think I am familiar with the proceedings; I have been deposed before a few times.* [Hint: too many words.]

Q: *Doctor, please speak a little slower, for the court reporter must record every word.*

A: *OK.*

Q: *In spite of your previous knowledge about deposition, I would like to give you a few general instructions so that it's clear for the record what the ground rules are, OK?*

A: *Fine, thank you.*

Q: *First of all, only one of us should talk at a time. What that means is that if I am talking, you should not talk, and if you are talking, I should not talk. That rule will be violated at some point—it is inevitable—but let's try to adhere to it.* [During the deposition, the court reporter will stop two people if they are talking at the same time.]

Secondly, your response must be verbal; shrugs, nods of the head, "aha," and "yeah" get confusing on the record, so please make yourself clear.

If your ATTORNEY or any other counsel has an objection to one of my questions, please allow that counsel to state the objection before you answer, unless, however, you are instructed not to answer that question; answer it anyway and we will determine later on in some sort of court hearing whether my question was proper or not.

A: *Fine.*

Q: *Lastly, if you do not understand my question, please say so and I will attempt to rephrase it so it will be more understandable to you. If you go ahead and answer the question without indicating you have a problem with it, it will be presumed by me and presumable by others in this room that you understood the question.*

A: *Thank you.*

Q: *Do you understand all of these instructions, Dr. Expert?*

A: *Yes, I do.*

Q: *Fine. We will now continue with the questions. I am marking this paper exhibit "Witness-1"; have you seen this before?*

A: *Yes, I have.*

[The ATTORNEY interrupts again.]
ATTORNEY: *Is that the notice of deposition?*
A: *Yes, it is.*

After this preliminary, the deposition continues. Normally, the LAWYER spends time on your qualifications. There may be questions about experience, which you should try to anticipate before the deposition day. The ATTORNEY should have given the LAWYER a copy of your curriculum vitae to review before the deposition.

Anything you say at the deposition will, in all probability, be used at the trial. Listen carefully to every question and take a few seconds after the question is asked to think and then formulate an answer. "Think before you speak" is the best advice at this point.

It cannot be overemphasized that it is essential for you as an EXPERT to be truthful at all times. Speak calmly; try to answer all questions in complete sentences. By the same token, if you are replying to a question and the LAWYER cuts you off, be sure you state that you are not finished. If a question is not clear to you, repeat the question in other words and ask the LAWYER if that is the question to be answered. Be sure to check before you answer! An alternative is to ask the LAWYER to repeat the question; do not hesitate to have the question repeated again and again. You may say, "If I understand your question correctly, you are asking me . . ." and then restate the question in your own words.

If the LAWYER has a degree in your field, your ATTORNEY should so advise you. Sometimes the LAWYER will try to show off the fact that he or she knows more toxicology (or chemistry or physics, or any science) than you as the EXPERT. Avoid getting into the trap of who knows more. Stick to your points, and do not try to annoy the LAWYER or to be cute.

Some LAWYERS will ask a series of simple questions to set a witness into a rhythm of replying "Yes," "Yes," "Yes," and then toss in a ringer to get the witness off base. The witness may answer "yes" but really mean "maybe." Do not let the LAWYER upset you!

Always answer a question briefly, but be sure that the points you wish to make get on the record. At times, it may be necessary to elaborate on an answer. However, be careful not to volunteer information that is not asked for and thus give the LAWYER new avenues to explore. Also, be careful not to show off your knowledge and ramble on. Be sure to make it clear that you cannot answer when questions are asked outside of your field of expertise. If you think the question asked is a trick question, it is acceptable to state that you think so before attempting to answer.

If you are required to answer a question with only a "yes" or "no," do so. You can also say, "Yes, but this answer needs elaboration." Another approach is to say, "Yes, but . . ." A third possibility is to say, "Yes. However, I can explain that. . . ." Thus you go on record as showing that a simple "yes" or "no" does not give the complete story. If you do answer only with a "yes" or "no," avoid continuing with a lecture, or an excuse, or a rationalization. (During the trial, the judge may ask you to elaborate.) Avoid being belligerent in your response.

Do not guess; if you do not know an answer, you do not know. Do not be goaded into making a statement you do not believe. Some LAWYERS will say, "Make an educated guess," or even "Give an answer to the best of your recollection." This can be a trap to be used against you at the trial. A question similar to, "Doctor, based on your experience as a toxicologist, in a similar situation, would you . . . ?" must not be answered. It may also be a trap!

At the deposition, and possibly at the trial, you will be asked about dates. The important dates are when the ATTORNEY first approached you, when the ATTORNEY asked you to be a consultant (if that was the first assignment), and when you became the EXPERT for this case. The chronology should be known, and a list of all lawyers with whom you as EXPERT have been in contact on this case can be requested. If asked for a date, make sure you state whether you are giving an actual date or an approximate date; otherwise this lapse may haunt you during the trial. In a similar vein, not everyone can recall each and every fact. If you cannot remember, say so; no apology is necessary. By no means should you as EXPERT offer to "look something up." Where will you look this something up? Does this offer reveal the existence of records or notes not given to the LAWYER during the discovery period?

Avoid superlatives and words like "always," "never," and "absolute"; and "never" say, "There is absolutely no evidence."

Do not explain your thoughts on how you arrived at an answer, unless asked specifically. Above all, do not let the LAWYER put words in your mouth. There is no "off the record" for the testifying EXPERT.

Your ATTORNEY may not speak during the deposition except to object to a question (for the record). If an objection is made, stop talking at once and let the attorneys deal with the objection. How you should proceed after an objection must be discussed prior to the deposition with your ATTORNEY. Because the objection goes on the record, you may, if instructed, attempt to answer the question. Your ATTORNEY may be making the objection to alert you to a potential problem.

During a deposition, your ATTORNEY officially cannot advise you not to answer a question; often, however, the ATTORNEY does just that. This aspect is not totally clear, and you must then turn to your ATTORNEY for advice. If possible, you should state (for the record), "I will not answer on advice of counsel."

Other attorneys in the room, who also have a vested interest in the case, may also object to either a question or an answer. Do not be disconcerted. You do not need to answer on points of the law. In addition, there are times when other attorneys who are not present may serve written questions in a sealed envelope to be opened by the court reporter, who acts as an officer of the court, and who reads the questions and then takes down the answers verbatim.

The deposition can go on for a few hours or a few days. You as the witness have the right to ask for a break at any time. This is especially true if you get confused. The length of the break should be announced to all.

During the break, a witness may or may not speak to anyone. This must be determined prior to the deposition by your ATTORNEY. Often, after a break, the LAWYER will ask, "Did you speak to anyone during the break?" If you did, say so; do not equivocate. If you say yes, the LAWYER will ask what you talked about. The object here is for the LAWYER to see if you have been coached. The style of your answer may be more important than its substance. The LAWYER may even ask, "Did your ATTORNEY tell you what to say?" Your best response is, "Well, yes, she told me to tell the truth!"

The break gives you as the witness a chance to think over your answers to previous questions, and may help you decide if a correction should be made. If that is the case, go on record just after the break and make that correction. If possible, explain why you made the correction before the LAWYER asks you. No one is perfect; every EXPERT makes some mistakes during a deposition. It does no good to become upset.

At some later time, you will get a copy of the deposition verbatim. Read it carefully in light of any new knowledge. Make any corrections in the margins or on a separate page. Some court reporters expect you to notarize any corrections you may make. On the draft deposition, some states permit you to draw a line through that which you wish to correct; other states do not. However, no erasing is permitted. Be assured any correction (except spelling) will be brought up in the courtroom during the trial; the objective is to help nullify your testimony. If the deposition is lengthy, your ATTORNEY's paralegal may be asked to compile an index, so during the trial the points in question can be found easily. The paralegal can be most helpful here in making both an index and a summary of the deposition for the ATTORNEY, and, of course, sending a copy of each to you.

WHAT DO YOU BRING?

You as EXPERT are expected to bring all documents previously requested by the LAWYER, sometimes even handwritten notes. Once in a while, the LAWYER who subpoenaed an EXPERT will expect the EXPERT to bring copies of previous depositions he or she has given, and even copies of his or her testimony in other trial cases. All of these may become exhibits for the trial. Arrangements should be made for the eventual return of the materials.

The ATTORNEY should see all documents before the deposition is taken. If it is not possible to show the ATTORNEY all documents before the deposition, it is best, when asked for the publications, to hand these to the ATTORNEY, who in turn will glance at each document and then will give each to the LAWYER. Some toxicologists will state that they know the field so well that they did not use any publications. This is permissible.

The transcript of the deposition, in the main, becomes public domain; almost anyone can pay to obtain a copy. Some court reporters will only sell copies to "authorized people." This does not matter; it is easy to obtain a copy.

CAN YOU USE REFERENCES?

At times you as EXPERT may rely on a special reference to give a correct answer to a question. That reference may already be marked as an exhibit; if not, the LAWYER may (or may not) wish to give it an exhibit number. If the reference is not marked as an exhibit, the ATTORNEY may make a note to be sure it is entered into evidence at the trial.

Exercise judgment about the use of references at the deposition (and even at the trial). If the LAWYER reads a quotation to you, you should ask to to see the original document before commenting. In one case, however, a judge ordered an EXPERT to comment on a quotation read by a LAWYER without letting the EXPERT see the original statement. Use of references during a deposition or trial must first be discussed with the ATTORNEY.

CAN YOU TAKE NOTES?

The question of taking notes should be thoroughly discussed with the ATTORNEY before a deposition. Taking notes is in general not a good idea, because it can be misunderstood. The question will be, Why is the EXPERT taking notes? What will they be used for? The LAWYER will certainly ask to see the notes; they may end up as an exhibit and may even appear at a trial.

One disadvantage to taking notes is that your ATTORNEY may not have a chance to see what you have written and thus study its effect on the case. Another disadvantage is that your notes may give the LAWYER new ideas and hence new approaches to the problem. There is also a chance that if you as the EXPERT take notes, the LAWYER can use words in the notes to try to undermine your credibility as an expert.

Chapter 10

The Courtroom: The Judge and Jury

If possible, while the court is not in session, it is best for the EXPERT to see the actual courtroom; it can be helpful in putting him or her at ease. Any information given to the EXPERT about the judge and jury can make him or her more effective during the trial.

PHYSICAL APPEARANCE

The EXPERT should not walk into completely strange surroundings, but he or she cannot be in the courtroom during the trial (in most instances) before he or she is called. If the EXPERT cannot be shown the actual courtroom, the ATTORNEY should explain in detail the physical layout of the room. A diagram or sketch would be helpful. The EXPERT witness should know where the judge sits relative to the doors. If one walks into the room, is the judge's area straight ahead, or left, or right? The jury box should be described. Where is it relative to the judge's seat? Where is the witness box? Will there be a microphone for the witness? Is drinking water available?

PROBLEMS WITH THE ROOM OR LAYOUT

If the EXPERT has any problem with the room itself or the layout, the ATTORNEY should be notified at once. For example, if the EXPERT wishes to have a table next to his or her chair for a briefcase or a small exhibit, this should be arranged before the EXPERT takes the stand. The ATTORNEY should see to it that water is available for the EXPERT. The EXPERT will have a problem if the witness box is too far from the jury or if it does not offer a clear view of the jury area for the EXPERT to see each member clearly. Arrangements of exhibits and the chalkboard must be thought out; neither of these should obscure the EXPERT's view of the jury.

WHAT TO EXPECT

The EXPERT will be called to the courtroom sometime after the trial has begun. Because he or she must remain out of the room until called, the ATTORNEY should have someone, perhaps a paralegal assistant, keep company with the EXPERT.

The EXPERT should be told how the judge conducts the court. What does the judge prefer; does the judge insist on short answers, or will he or she permit a witness to ramble on? Does the judge permit, or require, or forbid the members of the jury to take notes? Does the judge ask questions? Is the judge friendly, hostile, or aloof—especially in this case? Is the judge knowledgeable about the subject? Should the EXPERT take special precautions in educating the court on the merits of the case at hand?

What is the composition of the jury as to age, gender, and ethnic, cultural, and educational background? Do the jury members appear to be alert? Is there any problem with a specific jury member?

THE JUDGE TAKES OVER

Judges come from varied educational and social backgrounds. The vast majority are not well versed in science, let alone toxicology. One can assume that just about all judges have both college and advanced law degrees. Many are very interested and will follow testimony carefully. Some will ask questions of the EXPERT to elicit clarification. If this happens, the EXPERT should always speak directly to the judge and always address the judge as "Your Honor." The judge may be more interested in the content of the testimony of the EXPERT than the jury. Very seldom will a judge show off his or her knowledge.

There have been occasions when a judge has engaged an EXPERT in a conversation remote from the case at hand. For example, during a trial on the flammability of roofing tar paper, the judge engaged the EXPERT in a discussion of the chemistry of tar paper. This subject was not relevant to the case, but the judge seemed to want the audience in the courtroom to appreciate his knowledge of chemistry. In such cases the EXPERT must "play it by ear." It is important to recall that the 1992 Supreme Court decision gives the judge great latitude in allowing or disallowing evidence to be heard by the jury.

Some judges are uncomfortable with, or are even suspicious of, science and scientists. One famous judge in New York, who was responsible for judging class action suits of a very large nature, once said at a symposium:

> An expert can be found to testify to the truth of almost any factual theory, no matter how frivolous. . . . At the trial itself, an expert's testimony can be used to obfuscate what otherwise may be a simple case. . . . Juries and judges can be, and sometimes are, misled by such experts-for-hire.

Occasionally, an EXPERT witness will find the judge in a case to be prejudiced against the very case on which the EXPERT is expressing an opinion. This situation can become a form of harassment of the EXPERT. Judges have been known to prevent EXPERT witnesses from responding to questions posed by the ATTORNEY, possibly as a result of improper qualification of the EXPERTS by the ATTORNEY.

Judges can make unwise decisions, but that is not the concern of the EXPERT; no one should argue with the judge, no matter how tempting it is. The lawyers can and should deal with this aspect; if necessary, the ATTORNEY can appeal the judge's decision to a higher court. If the judge is giving the EXPERT a hard time, it is wise for the EXPERT to remain polite. The jury is negatively influenced by a witness who loses his or her cool; they expect that the EXPERT will be polite at all times when speaking to the presiding judge.

The judge has great leeway in running the courtroom and the case. The judge may have had prospective members of the jury answer special interrogatories intended to make them focus on the specific facts of the case. In doing so, the judge has hoped that the jury will understand the facts and thus be less likely to arrive at a compromise verdict. The judge wants the jury to make its decision during deliberation based on the preponderance of evidence. Unless the interrogatories are worded carefully, they may confuse the jury. Some judges allow jurors to take notes; if so, the EXPERT should speak much more slowly. In fact, some judges issue loose-leaf binders to jury members. Also, the judge may instruct lawyers to furnish written material to the court to be distributed to the jury members. In some states, the judge will require that the EXPERT file the opinion in writing prior to the trial, and then during the trial will require the EXPERT to read that opinion verbatim. Other judges forbid members of the jury to take notes.

In all cases, it is wise for the EXPERT to look at the judge occasionally while answering the questions posed by the ATTORNEY or LAWYER. Also, the EXPERT should look at the jury very often while answering questions, more than at the attorneys. (Not all attorneys agree with this strategy.)

Perhaps one of the most important facts for an EXPERT to keep in mind is that some judges, although they can be expected to be interested in the content of the EXPERT's testimony, have been known to rule in favor of or against cases on the demeanor of the witnesses and not at all on the science! Some judges have accepted the testimony of the EXPERT who is most adamant (although perhaps wrong) over that of the EXPERT who admits that there can be limits to the science under discussion.

At the end of the testimony, the EXPERT may hear the judge instruct the jury with the following statement: "You are the judge of the facts, but I am the judge of the law. It is your obligation to apply the rules of the law as I define them to the facts as you find them." Another judge may say: "You have heard evidence in this case from witnesses who testified as EXPERTS. The law allows EXPERTS to express opinions on subjects involving their special knowledge, training, skill, experience, or research. You shall determine what weight, if any, should be given such testimony, as with any other witness."

THE JURY AND YOU

The jury of six, eight, or twelve persons looks to the EXPERT as occupying a specific role: to help them decide which scientific facts are correct and which theories to believe. The toxicology EXPERT, therefore, plays a very important role.

Some members of the jury may be influenced by the television caricature of the scientist. So often, on the screen, the scientist is portrayed as a socially inept, inarticulate stereotype of the absent-minded professor. For this reason appearances are of paramount importance for the testifying EXPERT. Some juries (like some judges) are more interested in personalities than in either the facts of the case or the interpretation of the science. Juries can be prejudiced against an EXPERT who dresses in a very unconventional style. The EXPERT's dress should therefore be conservative. No outlandish ties or socks should be worn. Fancy rings should be removed. How can a playboy or playgirl appearance be taken seriously? Certainly a person has a right to wear what he or she likes, or what is comfortable. However, if the EXPERT wears jeans, in all likelihood the jury will not take his or her testimony too seriously.

After the EXPERT is called, he or she should walk to the witness stand with a bearing that radiates confidence, but not a cocky attitude, and make him- or herself comfortable. After sitting, the EXPERT should take a second to acknowledge the judge, then look at the jury before the oath is administered.

The EXPERT should avoid stacking the witness box table with papers, books, legal pads, or even sweaters. These create a physical barrier between the EXPERT and the jury. If books and the like are to be used, they should be in a briefcase or box and stored on the floor or a side table near the EXPERT. The hands should be visible, not in pockets. When speaking, the EXPERT may use his or her hands, but should avoid pointing a finger at any person.

At all times the EXPERT should project a relaxed appearance. Should the EXPERT have any special mannerisms, such as pulling his or her ear under stress, or a tremor of the hands, they should be disguised, if possible. If the ATTORNEY still wishes that this person appear as an EXPERT at the trial, the problem should be dealt with up front, prior to the start of the direct examination. For example, the following conversation may take place:

> **ATTORNEY:** *Dr. Expert, before we begin, I notice you have a slight tremor in your right hand. Is there any reason that you feel you cannot continue with my questions and the opposing LAWYER's cross-examination?*
>
> **A:** *It is certainly okay to continue. This slight shaking is an inherited trait in my family, and I really do not notice it. Please continue; let us both ignore it.*

Qualification comes next. The jury wants an EXPERT who can acknowledge his or her accomplishments without playing at false modesty or being overbearing: "Yes, I am the best in the world."

Some juries have been influenced by the age of the EXPERT, especially if two opposing EXPERTS differ on their conclusions and are obviously in different generations. The ATTORNEY must give some thought to this fact.

When you are on the witness stand, eye contact with members of the jury is very important, although you should occasionally answer a question while looking at the judge; other times look at the ATTORNEY who is asking questions. However, the most important lesson to learn is to remember that *the only real audience in the courtroom is the jury.*

Your ATTORNEY will start the questioning. Your answers should be to the point and as nontechnical as possible. Do not talk down to the jury. Do not patronize them. Assume the jury members are intelligent, are eager to do their civic duty, and wish to learn, but are uninformed. Some members are sensitive to being looked down upon and will take offense if they think an EXPERT implies that they are not too smart. Nonetheless, they will be aware that they are not knowledgeable on toxicology, or other particular scientific subject. Try to explain any complicated phenomena, and the problem at hand, as best you can in simple layman's language. Assume that the jury members have at least an eighth grade education. You must also demonstrate the validity of the analysis you are presenting, and above all, the logic of the conclusions. This duty has assumed greater importance since the *Daubert* ruling.

Problem Concepts

Excluding mathematical aspects, there are at least three concepts in the field of toxicology that must be carefully explained to a jury. These are the dose–response relationship, the phenomenon of *hormesis*, and the fact that a prediction of the toxicity of one inorganic compound from the known toxicity of a similar compound is totally unreliable. Even drawing a conclusion on the toxicity of an isomer of one organic compound from the known toxicity of another is tenuous. Examples include ethyl glycol versus propylene glycol.

The first concept follows from the basic tenet of the toxicologist: *The dose makes the poison.* A simple diagram (Figure 10.1) can be useful for explaining this concept, with the essential trace element zinc plotted against physiological status.

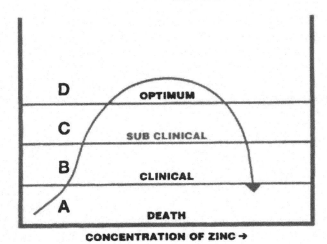

Figure 10.1   An example of changes in physiological status as the concentration (amount) of an essential element increases.

Zinc is called an essential trace element because no life can exist without it. More than 100 enzymes in the human body are zinc-dependent. One cannot breathe if no zinc is present in the lungs, because a zinc-dependent enzyme permits the dissolved CO_2 in the blood to be exhaled as CO_2 gas. Figure 10.1 shows that at no zinc or very low levels of zinc, no life exists (Box A). If a little more zinc is present, life can exist, but children born of zinc-deficient mothers may be dwarfed; the immune system, which protects humans from disease, does not function well (Box B, clinical symptoms). A little more zinc is helpful, but inadequate levels of zinc are related to an inability to taste and smell properly and to slow healing of wounds (Box C, subclinical symptoms). Adequate amounts of zinc in the body bring humans to optimum levels of functioning (Box D).

However, if the level of zinc increases further, the curve starts downward to Box C again; now the immune system can again be compromised and fail to function properly. Too much zinc upsets the body's use of the essential element copper. If even more zinc is present, a person may suffer from fume fever; small, special tumors may appear in the lungs (Box B). Addition of still more zinc may force the condition into Box A, death.

The second concept that may be difficult for a jury to understand concerns pharmacological inversions and hormesis.[1] At times, when a prescription drug is taken, a patient may find that the medication produces an effect that is completely opposite from that for which it was prescribed. The counterpart has been shown in experimental animals. These are illustrations of pharmacological inversion,

---

[1]There is an organization devoted to collecting information from the literature on hormesis. The BELLE (Biological Effects of Low Level Exposures) newsletter is available from the University of Massachusetts School of Public Health in Amherst, Massachusetts.

which may occur as a response–time effect or response–dose effect. Phenobarbital has often been prescribed as a sedative, but animals and humans very often undergo an excited phase at first, before the sedation phase, when a single dose is administered. Some people get a high on tranquilizers; others get depressed on mood elevators. Alcohol is an example of a response–dose inversion; a low dose can give opposite effects from a high dose. Likewise, a low dose of pure caffeine decreases heart rate, whereas a high dose moderately increases it.

What is not well known is that an accepted "toxic" agent at high or ambient level can actually be beneficial at a very low dose. Hormesis (derived from the Greek word *hormein*, meaning to excite or stimulate) is the term given to this phenomenon whereby an agent produces an adverse effect on a physiologic state at one dose level, but a beneficial effect at a much lower level. Many toxic metals are known inhibitors of enzymes, but at very low doses they stimulate the same enzymes. Cadmium is a known toxic metal with no known biological function, yet a low dose can stimulate growth and the activity of the enzyme catalase.

Arsenic in low doses stimulates growth of domestic animals and chickens; at higher doses, it retards their growth. Nickel is an essential element for some species; at higher doses, this element induces cancer.

Rats exposed to very low doses of X rays live longer than unexposed controls; at high doses, X rays induce malignancies. Mice, rats and dogs exposed to low levels of chloroform survive longer than controls; at high levels, tumors are induced by the same chemical.

The third concept that is difficult to relate to a jury is the unpredictability of the toxicity of one inorganic compound by comparison with a similar one. The LD_{50} of a cation is often determined by anions. The differences in the value of the acute toxicity between compounds of the same element can vary over a

Table 10.1 Relative Carcinogenicity
of Nickel Compounds in Rats

Nickel compound	Relative carcinogenicity
Ni_3S_2	100
NiS (crystalline)	100
NiO	93
NiS_2	86
Ni (powder)	65
NiSe	50
NiS (amorphous)	12
$NiCrO_4$	6
NiAs	0
$NiTiO_3$	0
$NiCl_2$	0

Note. All compounds given intramuscularly in the same strain of rats.

Table 10.2 LD$_{50}$ of Vanadium Compounds (mg/kg)

Compound	Rat	Guinea pig	Mouse
Vanadium pentoxide	1–2	20–88	87–117
Sodium vanadate	—	30–48	100–150
Ortho vanadate	2–3	1–2	58–100
Pyro vanadate	3–4	1–2	25–58
Tetra vanadate	6–8	18–20	25–58
Hexa vanadate	30–40	40–50	100–150

Note. All compounds given intravenously.

wide range. Major differences will be noted among species. Tables 10.1, 10.2, 10.3, and 10.4 give examples.

As mentioned, many scientific concepts can be explained in terms that the average person can understand. For example, risk assessment can be stated as "the risk of getting cancer after exposure is "2×10^{-4}." Risk can also be explained thus: "It is possible that two out of 10,000 people may be affected after being exposed to a chemical; this does not mean that two people out of a group of 10,000 will actually develop cancer if exposed." Thus, risk assessment must be understood by a jury as a guess as to what the possibilities can be.

Problem Terms

During a discussion of toxicology and levels of exposure, or dose received, many abbreviations are commonly used. Among these are: LD$_{50}$, ED$_{50}$, LC$_{50}$, TD$_{50}$, TLV, TWA, NOAEL, CERULA, TSCA, FIFRA. There are many other terms in common use by various branches of toxicology that may be mentioned by an EXPERT in the course of a trial. The testifying toxicologist must be prepared to define these terms in as simple language as possible or must give the jury simple synonyms. Included among these terms are: adducts to hemoglobin or DNA; apotosis, or cell death; DNA damage and repair; oncogenes;

Table 10.3 LD$_{50}$ of Lead Compounds (mg/kg)

Compound	Species	LD$_{50}$
Arsenate	Rat	100
Naphinate	Rat	5100
Nitrate	Guinea pig	1300
Chloride	Guinea pig	2000
Fluoride	Guinea pig	4000
Oleate	Guinea pig	8000

Note. All compounds given orally.

Table 10.4 LD$_{50}$ of Antimony Compounds in Rats (mg/kg)

Compound	LD$_{50}$	Antimony equivalence
SbO	100	100
Sb$_2$O$_3$	3250	1360
Sb$_2$S$_3$	1000	360
Sb$_2$S$_5$	1500	450

Note. All compounds given intravenously.

oncogene suppressor genes: p^{53}, APC, WT1, and others; slow and fast acetylators; sister chromated exchange; unscheduled DNA synthesis; Ah receptor; bioaccumulation; biomarkers; oxidative damage and free radicals; peroxisome proliferation; cytochrome P$_{450}$ and its isoforms; free radicals and singlet oxygen; gene expression; and transgenetic animals.

Jury–EXPERT Problems

Although this last section anticipates the next chapter on the actual trial procedure, it is placed here to call attention to some of the main jury–EXPERT problems.

Some juries are suspicious of an EXPERT whose practice is limited to testifying for the defense. (For some reason, an EXPERT who testifies only for a plaintiff, in the minds of some jury members, is not suspect!) The ATTORNEY must bring this misgiving into the open at an appropriate time. Some juries are not uncomfortable with an EXPERT whose sole source of income is testifying; but other juries ask, "Doesn't the EXPERT witness have a 'real job?'"

Many juries also take a negative view of the EXPERT who hangs around in the courtroom, after giving testimony. "Hasn't the EXPERT anything more important to do?" a juror may ask. Another juror may wonder, "Does the EXPERT have a financial stake in the outcome of this trial?" If the EXPERT does not leave after his or her testimony, other questions may come to the minds of jurors: "Is the EXPERT still being paid while sitting in the courtroom?" or "Is this person only a professional witness?"

To keep such questions from being raised, as soon as the EXPERT is excused, he or she should nod to the judge and walk out of the courtroom! If for some reason the ATTORNEY wishes the EXPERT to remain in the courtroom after his or her testimony is over, the jury should be made aware that the ATTORNEY has asked the EXPERT to stay.

Chapter 11

The Trial Comes Eventually

A trial is an expensive process for resolution of disputes. An adjudicator (the judge) must consider the actual facts and then apply the law to reach a legal resolution of that dispute. The jury, the trier of fact, then makes the decision as to which party is right.

Attempts are being made to prevent or minimize the expense of court cases. One means is by arbitration. The rules on arbitration vary a good deal; however, EXPERTS are often called upon to speak at arbitration hearings. The ATTORNEY must explain the rules of such hearings and how they differ from trials.

The EXPERT about to testify must be prepared for a long day. He or she should avoid all alcohol for at least a full day, get a good night's rest, and eat breakfast. When a case goes on to a trial, it can be tried before a judge alone or before a jury. In either case, the EXPERT must be prepared to be present at the time designated and perform the functions outlined in this book.

Occasionally, just before the trial date is reached, for some reason or other a trial is postponed. The ATTORNEY must notify the EXPERT of the postponement and when to expect the new trial. In case the ATTORNEY is negligent in this duty, the EXPERT should always call the ATTORNEY a few days before a trial to be sure the date is still firm. The EXPERT must be flexible as to dates, because the court and not the ATTORNEY determines the calendar for the rescheduled trial. At this point the EXPERT should inquire if the ATTOR-NEY needs another meeting or has additional information to give the EXPERT. Patience is important in this situation.

In most jurisdictions, the ATTORNEY must list the names of all EXPERTS who are to testify long before, or shortly after, a trial date is set. The ATTOR-NEY should notify the EXPERT when this event occurs. If a name of an EX-PERT is not listed, the judge can bar that EXPERT from testifying.

DIRECT EXAMINATION

The trial begins. The initial procedure is the same for most trials: You will be called to the witness stand. The bailiff or some officer of the court will ask you to raise your right hand, and to swear, promise, or affirm to tell the truth.

At all times, your body language is important, because it is a subtle form of communication. It tells a lot to the LAWYER. He or she will note how you answer—or refrain from answering—a question. What you do with your hands, what expression you have on your face, how you place your body forward, or how you sit slumped over are all telltale signs of your degree of comfort. Perhaps reading a book on the subject of body language may be useful.

You are the world's EXPERT and must act accordingly. Sit down and take a few seconds to adjust the seat and to adjust the microphone, if one is on the table, to about six inches from your face. Make yourself comfortable; you may be there a good many hours.

It is a good idea before you go on the witness stand to give the court reporters a list of technical words you may use, with their correct spelling. They will appreciate this gesture.

Your ATTORNEY now takes over and will ask you questions about your background. Your answers will let the judge decide if you qualify as an EX-PERT. The initial questions are almost pro forma. Expect questions like the following:

> **ATTORNEY:** *Your name?* [Answer and spell your name, so that "Dr. Expert" is on the record, not "Dr. Export."]
> **ATTORNEY:** *Your address?* [if necessary]
> **ATTORNEY:** *Your occupation—how long have you been employed?*
> **ATTORNEY:** *Tell the jury about your educational background.* [The ATTORNEY may say to the EXPERT, "Please give your answers to the jury, for they are the fact finders in this case."]

Give your educational information starting with undergraduate college. List all institutions of higher learning and the years you attended; also state your majors and the degrees obtained (and dates).

Some ATTORNEYS wish to speak this information themselves and merely have the EXPERT confirm it. For example: "You attended the University of

_____ during the years 1941 to 1945, did you not?" and "You received your MS in 1955 at the University of _____, is that correct?"

The qualification continues, with the ATTORNEY asking about your experience since graduating, your professional associations, offices held, research conducted, scientific papers published, and the like.

At the present time, there is some question about the importance of an EXPERT's publication record; it is therefore wise to mention some papers you have published in peer-reviewed journals. Emphasize *peer-reviewed*. You may be asked by the ATTORNEY to explain the meaning of peer review. Also, if you have published a paper related to the topic of the present court case, this fact should be highlighted for the jury.

All of this time, the court reporter will be taking all of your answers and statements down verbatim. Speak slowly, if possible. Many scientists get so involved in their testimony that their rate of speech may be too fast for the court reporter.

It is important for you as EXPERT to appear properly qualified for the jury to be duly impressed. This may take a good number of questions and much time. You may get bored during this procedure, but recall that these questions are for the judge and jury, not the LAWYER or the listeners who are sitting in the room. The questions will be similar to those at the deposition. As in the deposition, education and experience are the most important aspects of qualification. Both bragging and its opposite, false modesty, will be easily detected by the jury. The LAWYER may have questions, but this is rare at this stage. The judge makes the decision if you qualify as an EXPERT.

One very significant point: If you have a PhD or ScD and your ATTORNEY calls you "doctor," be sure the jury understands what your advanced degree is. Your ATTORNEY should ask you, "Dr. Expert, are you a medical doctor?" Your answer should be a simple "no." At this juncture, give no explanation. Then your ATTORNEY should ask you, "Why are you called 'doctor?'" You should explain to the jury that "doctor" is the appropriate title to address one who has attained that degree by virtue of completing advanced training. The doctor of philosophy or the doctor of science is different from the doctor of medicine. In the academic world, you should explain, the term "doctor" is commonly used to address a professor. Only if necessary, repeat information about your background that was used to qualify you as an expert witness.

Should your ATTORNEY fail to follow this suggestion, the LAWYER will have a field day during the cross-examination. If the different degrees are carefully explained during the qualification period, however, the jury will understand that the term "doctor" is not specific to the medical profession. This distinction is effective only if your ATTORNEY brings it out.

There may be times when the LAWYER will interrupt the listing of your qualifications and imply that, to save time, of course he or she will stipulate that you are an expert, and "let us continue with the trial." This offer should not be accepted by your ATTORNEY, who should continue to ask you about your scientific background. This information is important to impress the judge and jury. The reason the LAWYER attempts to stipulate that you are an expert is to prevent the jury from being impressed by your background.

Only after your qualifications are accepted by the judge and you are recognized as an EXPERT witness will the formal part of your testimony begin. The ATTORNEY will ask you a number of questions about the case. Many will be about the facts as you see them. Your answers should be made with sufficient certainty to let the jury know you are not equivocating. If you do equivocate, make that fact known. In your answers, avoid terms like, "I guess," "I think," and "I assume." At all times, be careful of any discrepancies between your deposition and your answers to questions at the trial. Remember, the ATTORNEY is the advocate, not you. This examination phase is to build up to the climax, "Do you have an opinion on the cause?" Your answer should be only one word, a simple "yes."

At this point, do not elaborate until asked to do so. You will have all the time in the world to explain your answer.

Some points to consider on direct examination: You are under oath and must answer all questions as truthfully as you can. When answering a question, do not even think of how your colleagues might react or criticize you for making the statements you do. Answer all questions briefly. Use lay language whenever possible. If you use technical terms, take a second to explain them. If the ATTORNEY asks the same question twice, assume that either you did not make yourself clear, or your answer was not what the ATTORNEY thought it should be. Do not repeat your former answer word for word; try to answer the question using different language, but keep the same thought.

Because you will have discussed the questions asked of you at this trial with your ATTORNEY beforehand, you will have formulated your answers prior to being on the witness stand. When making your preparations, decide which points you wish to make. Keep your weakest points in the middle of your answer; make your strongest point last. Juries will remember the last point you made, and they will also remember your weakest point if it is made at the very beginning of your reply.

Recall juries are interested in what you have to tell them. Consider that they are intelligent but uninformed; do not talk down to them. Assume that their education level is eighth- to twelfth-grade. All questions asked of you by your ATTORNEY in the jury's presence should be the same questions you and your ATTORNEY have discussed previously and even rehearsed during playacting. Your ATTORNEY will know your answers, but they are your answers. Again, the answers and the opinion are yours!

Occasionally, your ATTORNEY may spring a question on you that has not been previously discussed. Your answer may surprise the ATTORNEY. It is essential that for each question asked, the ATTORNEY knows the definite answer, although not necessarily its exact wording.

Juries feel uncomfortable with the EXPERT who always agrees with his or her ATTORNEY. Therefore your ATTORNEY and you may agree beforehand that he or she may ask some questions that require you to disagree mildly. Thus, during the direct examination by ATTORNEY, you should not hesitate to correct the ATTORNEY's question—and also to say "no," or "not exactly," or "That is not correct." This shows the jury that you are not just a "yes-person."

As in the deposition, any discussion you have with your ATTORNEY during the break or during lunch is "discoverable."

In this modern day and age, the judge and both attorneys may have laptop computers at their disposal. What you as the EXPERT say is taken down verbatim by the court reporter, as already noted. However, with the information superhighway, the hieroglyphics of the court reporter can possibly be translated into English in real time.[1]

A few hints to keep in mind during testimony: Never mention insurance; this may lead to a mistrial. Avoid mentioning the marital or sexual orientation of any other person.

SHOULD YOU USE NOTES?

As an EXPERT witness, you can refer to notes if necessary, but you should make proper explanatory remarks. Notes may be useful for placing exact dates and times on the record, or as examples of mathematical calculations. If you refer to notes too often, the jury may wonder how much you really know about the case; how much thought you have given to the problems of the case; how much you are relying on hints given to you; and how much real preparation you have made for the case.

At times, you may rely on books for specific information; these books must be made part of the evidence and have exhibit numbers. LAWYERS have been known to object to an EXPERT's referring to even a standard reference book such as *The Merck Index* if it has not been placed in evidence beforehand.

The LAWYER has a right to ask you to turn over to the court all notes and books used during your testimony. The books certainly will become exhibits. Do not neglect to let the court know that any books are to be returned after the trial is over; otherwise the books may get lost.

CROSS-EXAMINATION

The objective of cross-examination is to bring to the jury the points that the LAWYER believes will strengthen his or her case and weaken the ATTORNEY's case. Often this means that the LAWYER will try to nullify the testimony of the

---

[1]Two organizations are keeping track of testimony by experts: the Defense Research Institute in Chicago and the Association of Trial Lawyers of America in Washington, DC.

EXPERT. If it is not possible to negate that testimony, the next best strategy is to weaken it. Some LAWYERS will even attempt to disqualify the EXPERT.

The cross-examination is theoretically limited in scope to permit the LAWYER and, through his or her questions, the jury, to consider if the EXPERT is:

- familiar with the product or chemical;
- experienced in handling that agent;
- knowledgeable in all the literature and many textbooks where that product is described; and
- aware of all safety precautions regarding the product.

But the very first thing the LAWYER will certainly do is take advantage of any failure by the ATTORNEY to properly qualify you as an EXPERT, especially in distinguishing the PhD or ScD from the MD. In spite of the fact that the LAWYER already knows your true educational background, which will have been discussed during the deposition, the following exchange will undoubtedly take place before the jury:

> Q: *Dr. Expert.* [Note the sarcastic emphasis on the word "doctor." The jury may even detect a sneer on the LAWYER's face.] *I would like to go over your outstanding qualifications again.*
> A: *Fine.*
> Q: *Did you attend a medical school and receive the MD degree?*
> A: *No.*
> Q: *Did you ever intern in a licensed hospital?*
> A: *No.*
> Q: *Did you ever fulfill a residency that most all physicians undertake?*
> A: *No.*
> Q: *Are you licensed to examine a patient?*
> A: *No.*

Any witness in this situation cannot help but feel that he or she has been caught in a trap; facial and body language will display his or her inner feelings. Many members of the jury will note this. By this time the jury is wondering, "What kind of doctor is this Dr. Expert? In spite of the judge's accepting him or her as an EXPERT, did this doctor get his or her degree in a diploma mill? Shall we believe what this person says?"

So much of this negative "publicity" can be headed off by an alert, sophisticated EXPERT. Another set of answers can be:

> Q: *Dr. Expert.* [Note the emphasis on the word "doctor."] *What medical school did you graduate from?*
> A: *Mr.* [or Ms.] *Lawyer, I do not have a medical degree, but I do have a doctoral degree, called doctor of philosophy [science], best known as a PhD [ScD], from the University of _____.*

Q: *Have you ever interned in a licensed hospital?*
A: *No, I have not, but I did a postdoctoral research fellowship in toxicology at the University of _____ . This is special research training I completed after I obtained my advanced degree.*

At this point the LAWYER may decide to abandon this line of questioning and go on to another topic. Or the LAWYER may persist:

Q: *Did you ever fulfill a residency that most physicians take?*
A: *No sir [ma'am], but I have done research for a long period of time. I think that it is proper to point out that it takes more years of training to obtain a PhD than an MD.*
Q: *Are you board-certified in any medical specialty?* [Here the LAWYER may have an unexpected answer.]
A: *I certainly am. I am board-certified in toxicology. I am a diplomate of the American Board of Toxicology [a Fellow of the Academy of Toxicological Science]. As you know, the diplomate status is given to only the top members of the profession. We all know that board-certified professionals are the cream of the crop.*

These replies will do much to keep the jury aware that although you are not a medical doctor, you are well educated and legitimate as an EXPERT.

Another use for the cross-examination may be to make sure that certain studies, proposals, or conclusions of others are presented before the jury. The LAWYER's technique is to read an abstract or a portion of a study and ask you if you agree with it. Regardless of your opinion, the jury will have heard that abstract.

During cross-examination, remain objective and do not permit emotions to rise to the fore. This is difficult when one's integrity is questioned. It is important to be polite to the LAWYER and refrain from using sarcasm, or even humor. Be aware that the LAWYER may show or simulate hostility toward you. Answering in kind does not help your position. A dignified response is impressive under all circumstances; above all, keep your cool when before the jury. If you feel that your self-control may be slipping, a request to the judge for a short break will almost always be granted.

Be prepared to answer what may appear to be mundane, or even very personal, questions: "What were you hired to do?" "For whom did you work?" Some women may be asked, "Are you married?" If divorced, you may even be asked why.

The LAWYER may ask, "How many times have you testified in a trial?" and "How many times have you testified for the plaintiffs and how many times for the defense?"

When answering such questions, consider describing the time span; approximate dates are acceptable. Some EXPERTS have testified a number of times, but over a number of years; they do not necessarily appear to be professional witnesses. At any time, when appropriate, you may make it clear that you are a professional consultant, not a professional witness. A few states require that a testifying EXPERT must spend more time on professional activities than on testifying. The LAWYER will often follow up with a question about what percentage of your income is from testifying.

The LAWYER, or even the judge, may ask for dates, especially the date when you were first approached by your ATTORNEY; here you must be careful about the difference between first contact and when you were first asked to be a consultant, and then when you were designated to be the actual EXPERT in the case. A general question as to "when" can be confusing.

Another important set of dates may be requested by the LAWYER: "When did you arrive at your opinion? Give me a timetable of events and thoughts that led to your opinion. At what date did you tell your ATTORNEY that you arrived at your opinion?"

Not all LAWYERS ask for these dates, but be prepared before the jury to give these dates. When specific dates are requested, it is permissible to refer to a set of notes or a date book. This is accepted practice; no one is expected to have all important dates in his or her head. It is wise to keep a log of events leading up to your opinion.

Question after question will follow. The LAWYER may ask if you have brought the entire file with you to the trial. Unless you are under subpoena to bring that entire file, it is not necessary to do so. If the LAWYER tries to make a point that the entire file is not present, simply remind the LAWYER that the portion needed for the testimony is there. If the LAWYER had wanted the entire file, it would have been brought to court, but the LAWYER never requested it.

Is there a limit to the myriad questions the LAWYER can ask? The rule is that the LAWYER on cross-examination is limited to those points brought up in direct questioning. However, a good LAWYER can get around this rule by listening carefully to the information presented by the EXPERT in answering the ATTORNEY's questions.

During cross-examination, listen carefully to the LAWYER; sometimes the strategy the LAWYER is using to negate your testimony will be apparent. If the LAWYER poses a question on fundamental principles, you may agree, but be wary of a correlation that is not germane to the case under trial. It is important to disagree without getting into an argument, so that the LAWYER cannot tell the jury that you are an advocate and not an impersonal, independent witness. Other LAWYERS use questions that require a limited, but not complete answer; much worse, some pose questions with many clauses, qualifying adjectives, and adverbs. Do not hesitate to ask the LAWYER to clarify the question(s), and stick only to the facts. Any problems with awkward questions can be clarified on redirect examination by an alert ATTORNEY.

You and the ATTORNEY should try to predict before the trial what trick questions the LAWYER may ask. Everyone is familiar with the old ploy, "Have you stopped beating your wife?" In a trial, the question may be, "Have you ever lied?" The best answer is "Never under oath!"

Be careful of double negative questions. Another common tactic is for the LAWYER to pause and gaze at the witness after a brief reply to a question. Many EXPERTS feel pressure to say something in addition; do not succumb, for this can lead to problems.

As mentioned in the section about the deposition, it is best to avoid volunteering information beyond what answers are needed for the questions asked by either the ATTORNEY or LAWYER. If by chance you mention an extraneous topic, or if you elaborate too much and give too many examples in answer to a direct question, the LAWYER can bring these topics up in cross-examination. Diversions can be the subject of cross-examination. Remember, if you have ever written a paper for scientists or for the lay public, the LAWYER is free to ask about it without showing that paper to you.

There have been times when a LAWYER asked an EXPERT to comment on a scientific journal article not written by the EXPERT. You have every right to request a copy of that paper; you can take as much time as necessary to read and think about it.

One last major point to ponder: Many LAWYERS have cross-examined EXPERTS in such a way as to really enhance the LAWYER's case. This is because the LAWYERS are successful in confusing the EXPERT, twisting the interpretation of what the EXPERT says, or just outwitting the EXPERT.

In all probability, the LAWYER will have a laptop computer available. Because, as noted, all testimony is taken verbatim, and the transcript of the court proceedings can be available in real time, it may be possible for the LAWYER to scan back to a previous answer to a question and get the exact wording of the answer. This information will be used to try to "nail" you on any discrepancies. Any answer given during cross-examination that is not precisely the same as given before will be challenged. Thus, a sharp LAWYER can ask, "What prompted you to change your answer now? You gave a different answer to my question three hours ago." Keeping your head, it is best to admit that the answer given now is not precisely the same as your previous answer; but wasn't the new question different, or with a different slant or emphasis?

The LAWYER may also try to impeach your present testimony by quoting from your testimony in a different lawsuit. Even if he or she did not obtain the transcript from you during your deposition, he or she may have received it from other lawyers or organizations.

RE-DIRECT EXAMINATION

If the ATTORNEY believes the LAWYER has brought out certain points (or facts) that will either mislead the jury or make your original statements less clear, the ATTORNEY may wish to ask you further questions on redirect examination. Generally, new facts are not brought out at this time. The ATTOR-NEY may just wish to emphasize points made earlier in the direct examination. This is also the opportunity for the ATTORNEY to counteract any wrong impression made to the jury during the cross-examination. In other words, the redirect is to clear up various points that the ATTORNEY believes were left unclear.

RE-CROSS EXAMINATION

The LAWYER has one more chance to soften the effect of the EXPERT on the jury. As a rule, the re-cross must be confined to those aspects covered in redirect. New evidence and new types of questions are not permitted. It must again be emphasized that you as EXPERT should not elaborate too much when answering a question, because you may give the LAWYER an opening. If the ATTORNEY objects, the LAWYER can say, "But Your Honor, this is not a new topic; the witness said so and so."

Chapter 12

The Attack on You

Some of the material in this chapter has been covered in other parts of the book. However, for the novice testifying EXPERT it will be useful to have this material reiterated.

As mentioned, during the cross-examination, the LAWYER will attempt in any way possible to nullify the information you gave during both the deposition and the direct examination in court. The main objective of the LAWYER is to display you (and hence your opinion) to the jury in the most unfavorable light possible. Misleading questions are often used. Sometimes the LAWYER will say or insinuate that you came to your opinion hastily, without considering all facts and factors of the case. You must be prepared for this accusation.

In some cases, the LAWYER will be abusive. You must, at all costs, keep your cool. If you as EXPERT are polite at all times, this action can sometimes defuse a vicious attack, or cause it to backfire on the hostile LAWYER. One hint: Avoid looking at your ATTORNEY when answering a question posed by the LAWYER. The jury or judge will think you are looking to the ATTORNEY to give you a clue or to see if your ATTORNEY accepts or rejects your answer. Also, avoid humor and sarcasm.

ATTEMPTS TO DISQUALIFY

There are at least three fronts on which a LAWYER can attack an EXPERT: credibility, integrity, and testimony. The LAWYER will try to convince the jury that you have given your opinion without adequate forethought, that the opinion was a snap judgment. Another technique used by the LAWYER is to get you to make a "laundry list" of the facts in the case. Following the presentation of this list, the LAWYER will tell the jury that you have left out an important reference. "How can a real EXPERT forget this very important point?" The implication is that you are unaware or unsure of important facts. The challenge for you is to avoid getting flustered.

Some LAWYERS will try to make you give a single citation on which you relied to form your opinion. This is an attempt to prevent the jury from hearing that you conducted an extensive literature search before forming the opinion. An alternative ploy is the LAWYER to ask, "Are these the only references you can find? Are you sure you have not overlooked an important reference found in the literature?"

Sometimes a LAWYER will bring a textbook to the trial and quote a passage from that book that apparently disagrees with you. You should immediately explain that textbooks are written to teach principles and the information in them is not applicable in all cases. Another ploy is for the LAWYER to read a sentence, or part of a sentence, from your deposition, and then ask, "Do you still agree with that statement?" Sometimes a LAWYER may even ask, "Did you lie when you answered my questions at the deposition?"

The LAWYER can quote his or her own EXPERT and say or imply that the ATTORNEY's expert is not as familiar with the facts as is the LAWYER's. Another ploy is for the LAWYER to listen to your answer and then cut you short, thus permitting the jury to hear only part of your testimony. In this situation, you should appeal to the judge to be permitted to finish the answer. At this point, you should make eye contact with various members of the jury.

The LAWYER can question the validity of the results of any test or experiment conducted that is damaging to his or her case. The LAWYER can force you to discuss the test in great detail. If you hesitate or hedge on any point, the LAWYER will use this opportunity to try to throw doubt on your scientific competence. At times, some LAWYERS will avoid asking any questions of substance for fear of getting damaging answers.

YOUR PREVIOUS PUBLICATIONS AND STATEMENTS

Long before the trial, you should have acquainted the ATTORNEY with any publications you have written that can even remotely be related to the present case. With the sophisticated databases available, the LAWYER can get a complete list of your published work. There are also companies that can furnish photocopies of any or all of your publications.

Some LAWYERS have confronted EXPERTS during cross-examination with statements made during public speeches. It is even possible that private conversations will be the subject of questions posed by the LAWYER.

YOUR PREVIOUS TESTIMONY

The LAWYER can usually obtain copies of all depositions and court records in which you have testified. Of course, you should have reviewed with the ATTORNEY any statement made previously that could have some bearing on the case at hand. If there is some potentially embarrassing statement in your earlier testimony, you and the ATTORNEY must decide how, within scientific integrity, you can explain it. If new information has appeared after the previous statements, conclusion, or opinions were recorded, be prepared to cite chapter and verse.

It should be emphasized for the court that ideas are dynamic and not static. You may have testified previously that there is no human counterpart that can be related to the findings from certain animal tests. However, new information may have come to light that required you to change your mind about the safety or lack of safety of a substance. This information could have come from new publications or even from unpublished data related by a scientific colleague! This possibility should be explained carefully, without giving the jury the feeling that you are defensive on this subject.

As mentioned previously, the LAWYER will undoubtedly ask you again and again how many times you have testified in court. At this point, the LAWYER may also ask what percentage of these cases were for the plaintiff and what percentage for the defense. A favorite question of a LAWYER is, "What percentage of your yearly income is from testifying in court cases?" In any case, the LAWYER will try, by direct statement or innuendo, to convince the jury that you are not unbiased, but philosophically favor one side over another. Along this line of questioning, the LAWYER may ask, "How many times have you testified [or evaluated cases] for your present ATTORNEY? Were these cases similar to this one? If you did not testify for this particular ATTORNEY, did you do any work for another attorney in that ATTORNEY's law firm?"

WHO AGREES WITH YOU OUT THERE?

What should you do or say if the LAWYER demands that you answer the question, "Who agrees with you out there?"

This type of question can be a real problem. There are competent, honest scientists who do not believe or agree with other competent scientists on generally accepted scientific inference. Because EXPERTS must interpret and have opinions on the facts of a case, it is not surprising that they disagree. Facts are often imprecise, and perceptions of facts often depend on mindset. As has been said, we hear what we want to hear and see what we want to see. Some scientists will state their disagreements openly. For example, some vocal scientists do not believe the pathological condition of AIDS has the HIV virus as its causative agent. If you as EXPERT are asked to name names of those scientists who agree with your opinion or conclusion, there should be no problem naming other scientists whose views are in the public domain. Those agreeing scientists may have written or given public speeches expressing their views.

The dilemma comes when you as EXPERT cite the views of some scientists, which, although carefully thought out, do not follow mainstream science. There are scientific controversies in which scientists disagree with "common knowledge," but do not speak up because it is politically unwise to make their views known in public (possibly because of potential funding consequences). An example is the issue of whether human lung cancer can be induced by "sidestream" or "second-hand" or "environmental" tobacco smoke (ETS). Many reputable scientists do not believe the government has made a strong case to regulate ETS as a group A carcinogen, but they do not choose to make their views known publicly.

At the present time it is accepted dogma that chloroform in drinking water, or chloroform absorbed by the body from shower water, is a causative agent for cancer in humans. Not all scientists agree, but the U.S. government has declared that chloroform is a carcinogen.

There is no agreement on the extent to which environmental chemicals are primary causes of human cancer. There are still questions on how realistic the government's decision is not to accept threshold doses for carcinogens. Mathematical risk assessment techniques can be employed to determine the number of people who potentially will get cancer if exposed to different dose levels, although different mathematical models can give results different in magnitude. It cannot be stressed enough that statistics apply to a population, not a specific individual.

Although not a toxicological problem per se, the use of DNA "fingerprinting" to identify a specific individual is another area of some disagreement. Is the accepted accuracy of fewer than two false positives per 1 million correct?

If you do know firsthand of the unconventional views of a scientist out there, there is no choice, under oath, but to answer truthfully, even though you may create hard feelings later among the scientists named. You and the ATTORNEY must have a prior discussion on what is hearsay. (Obviously, there is no problem naming scientists who do accept the mainstream conclusions, even though many of those agreeing have never done research in that particular field.)

When Experts Disagree

There are times when experts disagree on actual facts, and more often on the conclusions that should be reached after the facts are studied and evaluated. This is a legitimate part of science; there is not always unanimity on interpretation, especially if two experts disagree on the facts presented in a case.

The LAWYER may ask your opinion about his or her EXPERT who gives a contradictory opinion. The LAWYER may ask, "Isn't Dr. X well known?" Your answer may be "yes" or "no." The next question will be, "Doesn't Dr. X have a good reputation in the field?" It is possible to answer the question of the reputation of the opposing EXPERT in various ways.

One possible statement is, "Counselor, it is not my duty to qualify your witness." Another, less brusque, answer is, "Counselor, your expert is known to me; I have respect for him [or her], but in this case, I strongly disagree with his [or her] opinion." Another approach is to say that "Dr. X is a good scientist, but really is not accepted as an expert in this particular field. In any event, I am not belittling Dr. X or his reputation."

If you are aware of who the opposing EXPERT is, it is not wise to make disparaging remarks about him or her. Some courts have ruled that it is not proper to impeach a witness until that person has had a chance to testify. In the long run, when there is a battle of the EXPERTS, the jury declares the victor. If you foresee a problem with the opposing EXPERT, see if your ATTORNEY will permit you to be present when his or her deposition is taken so that you can learn what reports that person has written. A highly charged buzz contention is that "No honest expert can disagree with my conclusion." The jury must be made aware that this statement is phony.

Problems with the Iconoclast

Both the ATTORNEY and LAWYER will have a problem with the EXPERT who offers an unorthodox explanation for a scientific phenomenon. Many scientists may not follow mainstream thinking and can offer an alternative theory; other scientists may merely present "off the wall" hypotheses. Both you and the ATTORNEY must analyze with open minds any unorthodox statements and make major decisions: Are these explanations potentially valid? Are they just junk science? Also, different states have different attitudes on permitting nonscientists to testify. These laws are important when a court can rule that hard science is not the main problem, such as in cases requiring a handwriting expert or document examiner.

Your function as an EXPERT is to give the court the benefit of your thoughts, reasoning, and conclusion. Be honest with the court and yourself. If you have respect for an iconoclast, you should so state clearly, but it is nonetheless possible to disagree.

If you believe an iconoclast is equal to "Dr. Moonbeam," state your opinion to the jury unemotionally, without rancor or even humor. It is not a good idea just to laugh at Dr. X. It is important to attack Dr. X's logic and reasoning and not Dr. X him- or herself, even if Dr. X is "out of this world." If possible, explain to the jury what is wrong when Dr. X disagrees with mainstream science, or when Dr. X gives a global statement (or prediction) that turns out not to be true (or is idealistic, but not based on fact).

At all times, be careful and be aware that the iconoclast may in the long term be right. At no time should any EXPERT underestimate the opposing EXPERT.

INADMISSIBLE OR QUESTIONABLE EVIDENCE

As an EXPERT, you must walk a tightrope in the area of evidence. Some ATTORNEYS try to insert inadmissible evidence into the framing of hypothetical questions. You should resist the request of the ATTORNEY to introduce inadmissible evidence (if you are aware of it) under the guise of explaining the reason behind an opinion. However, you are free to base an opinion on inadmissible material if it is reliable. Again, a sharp line must be drawn; such an opinion is limited as to its use in court. Some LAWYERS may try to get you to answer a question in such a way that inadmissible, or questionable, evidence is touched upon.

THE ABUSIVE SITUATION

Not too often, but occasionally, this situation has occurred: The LAWYER not only deals with an EXPERT in a hostile manner, but actually becomes verbally abusive. The LAWYER may inquire about the EXPERT's personal life, especially finances, or even allude to sexual behavior. More often than not, the abusive LAWYER will try in any way possible to make the EXPERT uncomfortable. This can be done, especially during the deposition, by making the room uncomfortable, delaying needed breaks, or otherwise trying to manipulate the proceedings so that the EXPERT will suffer real fatigue.

LAWYERS can ask insignificant questions, can be repetitive, and can be argumentative. They can ask personal questions not related to the case. They can attempt to force a witness either to render an opinion or elaborate on an opinion much beyond the actual situation or facts. Abuse can be subtle as well. One form of abuse is not to pay the fee or, under certain circumstances, to subpoena the EXPERT with no fee attached.

The LAWYER may shout at the EXPERT and, while looking at the jury, say something ridiculous, for example, "This so-called expert is the only one in the world who does not believe that water causes cancer!!!" Another technique an abusive LAWYER can use is to remind the EXPERT time and time again that the EXPERT is under oath; this technique insinuates to the jury that the EXPERT has a tendency to lie.

A witness has a right not be abused at the deposition or trial. Be definite and open in stating, in a polite manner, that the question asked is offensive. Above all, you can refuse to answer an abusive question; this must be done, if possible, without engaging in a mud-slinging contest. The EXPERT who gets into a fight with the LAWYER usually loses face with the jury, and the jury quite often may ignore this EXPERT's testimony. All this must be on the record;

in severe cases, you may terminate the deposition and leave the room. You must be absolutely correct in your evaluation of the abuse; otherwise, an erroneous termination may be costly to the case.

The ATTORNEY must be helpful here. If the LAWYER is known to engage in abusive behavior, the ATTORNEY must warn you; together you and the ATTORNEY must develop a strategy to deal with any expected abuse. As a last resort, if you believe you may be subject to a LAWYER's abuse, ask your personal attorney also to be present.

Notably, there have been times when the EXPERT has been the abuser; this type of abuse is often related to ethics. An EXPERT may have a contingent-fee service. An EXPERT might switch sides, or even give or sell his or her report to the opposing LAWYER. An EXPERT might withhold information from, or present false information to, the ATTORNEY or—much worse—the jury, resulting in an erroneous verdict. An EXPERT might falsify an experiment, or fail to conduct an experiment, or fabricate results. An EXPERT may not disclose all the opinions held or might fail to use all available data. Another form of abuse is when an EXPERT, although knowing better, gives long rambling answers designed to confuse a jury.

Chapter 13

The Aftermath

An EXPERT's obligation does not stop when the verdict is given by the judge or jury, or even if the judge dismisses the suit (summary judgment). There are many details yet to be completed.

YOUR RESPONSIBILITIES

An EXPERT must see to it that myriad details are taken care of and all tasks satisfactorily completed.

It is essential to contact the ATTORNEY after the trial or after testifying. If possible, you and the ATTORNEY should have a postmortem session in person. If this is not possible in a reasonable time, a courtesy letter is in order. You should thank the ATTORNEY (and vice versa) and, if there have been any problems in the relationship, include a diplomatic note suggesting possible remedies. Perhaps you can make a checklist of good and bad points and share it with the ATTORNEY.

At this time, it is wise to include any additional bills, and inquire when you can expect payment.

Too often, the ATTORNEY does not contact the EXPERT immediately at a trial's end to let the EXPERT know that a verdict was given. It is nice to learn if the ATTORNEY believes that the EXPERT's testimony had significant impact on the favorable outcome of a case.

If a particular case or trial appears to be unusual to you, or even to the ATTORNEY, you may consider writing an academic article describing the distinctive aspect of the case. The ATTORNEY must make the final decision as to whether an article is in order. No writing should be done until the final disposition of the case, after all appeals are completed. If you do not heed this warning and publish a "story" and the case is retried for any reason, this published article will place you in an unfavorable position.

WHAT PAPERS AND PROPERTY DO YOU KEEP?

There is no agreement on how long to keep papers and notes pertaining to your trial. Some EXPERTS keep everything forever. Others clear their files as soon as they know of the disposition of a case. One EXPERT has a five-year rule: If there has been no activity on a particular case for five years, then all materials pertaining to it may be destroyed. It is a good rule of thumb to keep all records at least until after all appeals have been resolved. Often a year may not be sufficient time for a possible new trial; thus, all papers pertaining to the case may have to be kept two years or longer. Some ATTORNEYS ask EXPERTS to return the papers. If this is the case, return all materials by certified mail, with return receipt requested. The receipt is your protection.

You must contact the ATTORNEY in regard to the disposal of any papers or property. If the ATTORNEY requests that you have all documents destroyed, the destruction of all papers must be in such a manner that they cannot be retrieved by anyone. A shredder is best, although personally taking the papers to the dump is acceptable. If possible, papers should be burned.

If the ATTORNEY says, "Do whatever you want with them," you must make a decision. Do you want to keep them all, or only a fraction? Recall that it is possible that these papers can be obtained by a future LAWYER through discovery in a different case.

It is a good idea, however, to keep copies of all your personal depositions. Also, keep a file on all the trials in which you were involved—their dates, their types, the sides for which you testified, and the names of the ATTORNEYS and firms.

SOME POSSIBLE NEGATIVE FEEDBACK

No matter on which side you have testified and offered an opinion, if there is publicity about the trial, some scientific colleague or other will be critical of your testimony. Often, the critics will get the facts wrong from the mass media, or will somehow have an incorrect perception of the testimony. Not all scientists will take the time to evaluate the validity of your testimony. A small minority will criticize not the science proposed, but the scientists for testifying.

If your testimony is on the "emotion of the day," a few may even wish to punish, or outlaw, or censor you. There have been times when an EXPERT has been verbally accused of scientific fraud because his or her testimony was not up to the critics' liking and did not fit the critics' prejudice. A testifying EXPERT must at all times "let the chips fall where they may."

WHAT THE FUTURE HOLDS FOR YOU

Your future as an EXPERT witness depends on a number of factors. Your relationship to the ATTORNEY is important. How well did you do at the trial? How useful were you to the ATTORNEY during the preparation of the case? Finally, much depends now on your willingness to be subjected to the tribulations of a trial again, to a LAWYER who may give you a hard time, and to a judge who may be unsympathetic.

Selected Bibliography

GENERAL BOOKS

There are only a few books that relate to the expert witness. Most are very general and emphasize the engineer or the medical doctor. None appear to be aimed at the toxicologist. Many are written for lawyers and therefore cite many court cases, rules, and laws. This bibliography contains books that may be helpful. No legal documents are included, nor are specific citations made to any of these references.

Bradley, M. D. 1983. *The scientist and engineer in court.* Washington, DC: American Geophysical Union.

Brownstein, D. A. 1993. *Law for the expert witness.* Ann Arbor, MI: Lewis Publishers.

Brushwood, D. B. 1986. *Medical malpractice pharmacy law.* Colorado Springs, CO: Shepard's McGraw-Hill.

Cranor, C. F. 1993. *Regulating toxic substances.* New York: Oxford University Press.

Feder, H. A. 1991. *Succeeding as an expert witness.* New York: Van Nostrand Reinhold.

Federal Judicial Center. 1994. *Reference manual on scientific evidence.* Edited by J. S. Cecil, C. E. Drew, M. Cordisco, and D. P. Miletich. Washington, DC: Federal Judicial Center.

Kennedy, R. D. 1983. *California expert witness guide.* Berkeley: California Continuing Education of the Bar.

Koppenhaver, K. M. 1990. *How to be a credible witness.* Available from Forensic Document Examiners, P.O. Box 324, Joppa, MD 21085.

Madden, M. S. 1992. *Toxic torts deskbook.* Chelsea, MI: Lewis Publishers.

Matson, J. V. 1990. *Effective expert witnessing.* Chelsea, MI: Lewis Publishers.

Nothstein, G. Z. 1984. *Toxic torts.* Colorado Springs, CO: Shepard's McGraw-Hill. [Shepard's McGraw-Hill also publishes supplements to G. Z. Nothstein's books.]

Poynter, D. 1987. *The expert witness handbook.* Santa Barbara, CA: Para Publishing.

Strodel, R. C. 1988. *Securing and using medical evidence in personal injury and health care cases.* Englewood Cliffs, NJ: Prentice-Hall.

Surosky, A. E. 1993. *The expert witness guide for scientists and engineers.* Malabar, FL: Krieger Publishing.

SPECIAL BOOKS AND BOOK CHAPTERS

Cecil, J. S., and Willging, T. E. 1993. Court-appointed experts: Defining the role of experts appointed under Federal Rule of Evidence 706. In *Reference manual on scientific evidence,* J. S. Cecil, ed. Washington, DC: Federal Judicial Center.

Chester, M. A., Sanders, J., and Kulmuss, D. S. 1989. *Social science in court.* Madison, WI: University of Wisconsin Press.

Clifford, R. C. 1991. *Qualifying and attacking expert witnesses.* Santa Ana, CA: James Publishing.

Edlavich, S. A., ed. 1992. *Pharmacoepidemiology.* Ann Arbor, MI: Lewis Publishers.

Hamlin, S. 1985. *What makes juries listen.* New York: Harcourt Brace Jovanovich.

Thomas, W. A., ed. 1974. *Scientists in the legal system: Tolerable meddlers or essential contributors?* Ann Arbor, MI: Ann Arbor Science Press.

USEFUL TOXICOLOGY BOOKS

There are a few large compendiums on toxicology, such as C. D. Klaassen, ed., *Casarett and Doull's Toxicology, The Basic Sciences of Poisons,* fifth edition, 1996; W. A. Hayes, ed., *Principles and Methods of Toxicology,* third edition, 1994; and A. M. Fan and L. W. Chang, eds., *Toxicology and Risk Assessment: Principles, Methods, and Applications,* 1996; as well as encyclopedias such as Ballantyne, Marrs, and Turner's two-volume set, *General and Applied Toxicology.* There are a plethora of toxicology journals. These are most familiar to toxicologists and therefore not listed here.

There are also large references that concentrate on medical aspects, like Gosselin, Smith, and Hodge's *Clinical Toxicology of Commercial Products,* and Ellenhorn and Barceloux's *Medical Toxicology: Diagnosis and Treatment of Human Poisoning.*

For handy references to toxicology, for the expert and even for those in related sciences, as well as attorneys, these four books can be recommended:

Loomis, T. A., and Hayes, A. W. 1996. *Loomis's essentials of toxicology.* 4th ed. New York: Academic Press.

Lu, F. C. 1996. *Basic toxicology,* 3rd ed. Washington, DC: Taylor & Francis.

Ottoboni, M. A. 1993. *The dose makes the poison,* 2nd ed. Berkeley, CA: Vincente Books.

Timbrell, J. A. 1995. *Introduction to toxicology,* 2nd ed. Washington, DC: Taylor & Francis.

SPECIAL PUBLICATIONS RELATED TO EXPERTS

More and more serials are constantly appearing, available by subscription, for the expert witness. Two that may be of interest are *Shepard's Expert and*

Scientific Evidence Quarterly, published by Shepard's McGraw-Hill, Clorad Springs, CO; and *Scientific Evidence Review*, published occasionally by the ABA Section on Science and Technology.

RELATED JOURNAL ARTICLES

In addition to books, there are a number of journal articles that deal in a general way with the expert witness.

Brown, A. L. 1986. Prediction in the face of uncertainty: The United States versus Reserve Mining Company. *Regulatory Toxicology and Pharmacology*, 6:75–79.

Connolly, D. R. 1986. Insurer perspectives on causation and financial compensation. *Regulatory Toxicology and Pharmacology*, 6:80–88.

Davidson, M. S. 1989. The limitations of scientific testimony in chronic disease litigation. *Journal of the American College of Toxicology*, 10:431.

Faust, D., and Ziskin, J. 1988. The expert witness in psychology and psychiatry. *Science*, 241:31–35.

Frankel, M. E. 1986. Causation and lawyers' causes. *Regulatory Toxicology and Pharmacology*, 6:89–94.

Furst, A. 1995. The Frye Rule is out: Is junk science in? *Journal of the American College of Toxicology*, 14:61–68.

Gots, R. E. 1986. Medical causation and expert testimony. *Regulatory Toxicology and Pharmacology*, 6:95–102.

Harter, P. J. 1986. Dilemma of causation in toxic torts. *Regulatory Toxicology and Pharmacology*, 6:103–107.

Jaffee, M. S. 1970. Expert witness. *Materials Research and Standards*, 10:8–11.

Kantrowitz, S. B. 1981. Expert testimony and scientific evidence—arson-related cases. *Journal of Forensic Science*, 26:142–152.

Kotin, P. 1986. Causation and financial compensation. *Regulatory Toxicology and Pharmacology*, 6:108–115.

Kovac, F. J. 1990. The role of the consultant in R & D. *The Chemist*, November:5–7.

Louis, D. E. 1982. Guidelines for expert witnesses. *Journal of the Air Pollution Control Association*, 32:1029–1030.

MacCoun, R. J. 1989. Experimental research on jury decision-making. *Science*, 244:1046–1050.

Mahoney, R. J., and Litlejohn, S. E. 1989. Innovation on trial: Punitive damages versus new products. *Science*, 246:1395–1399.

Morris, W. A. 1990. The chemist as an expert witness. *The Chemist*, 7:21.

Piehler, H. R., Twerski, A. D., Weinstein, A. S., and Donaher, W. A. 1974. Product liability and the technical expert. *Science*, 186:1089–1093.

Sherman, J. D. 1983. Women as expert witnesses: Trials and tribulations. *Trial*, August:47–48.

Sugarman, S. D. 1990. The need to reform personal injury law leaving scientific disputes to scientists. *Science*, 248:823–827.

Susser, M. 1986. Rules of inference in epidemiology. *Regulatory Toxicology and Pharmacology*, 6:116–128.

Wang, C. C. K., and Parker, H. E. 1984. How to be an effective expert witness. *Chemical Engineering News*, February 20:87–90.

SPECIAL ARTICLES

These articles are especially useful for the toxicologist:

Epstein, B. M., and Klein, M. S. 1987. The use and abuse of expert testimony in product liability actions. *Seton Hall Law Review,* 17:656–676.

Klein, M. S. 1990. Expert testimony in pharmaceutical product liability actions. *Food Cosmetic Law Journal,* 45:393–442.

Neal, R. A., and Doull, J. 1995. The discipline of toxicology. *Fundamental and Applied Toxicology,* 24:151–153.

VIDEOTAPES

The State Bar of Wisconsin (P.O. Box 7158, Madison, WI 53707-7158) has a series of videotapes for attorneys to help prepare an expert witness. These tapes are available to the public; the cost in 1993 was about $100.00 each. A list can be obtained by writing to the above address.

Index

Printed in the United States
by Baker & Taylor Publisher Services